THE MARY ANSWER

Embracing God's Disruptions and Detours

Chris Syme

CONTENTS

INTRODUCTION

*"Now faith is confidence in what we hope for and
assurance about what we do not see."*

HEBREWS 11:1

*"So here's what I want you to do, God helping you: take your everyday
ordinary life—your sleeping, eating, going-to-work, and walking-
around life—and place it before God as an offering. Embracing what
God has done for you in the best thing you can do for him."*

ROMANS 12:1 MSG

Superstars of real faith are rarely superstars in real life. They are ordinary people who believe in an extraordinary God. They are people who say "yes" to God's invitation to disrupt their lives because they have an undying faith in his unfailing love. They have confidence in the One they cannot see. They embrace whatever God asks them to do knowing that he is preparing them for something that will reveal his glory. God is giving you and I that same invitation to walk with him today. In this study you will see Romans 12:1-2 from The Message version referenced in many different contexts. Those verses are the cornerstone of Women Finishing Well and the place where the conversation about embracing disruption starts.

In this book we will look at the lives of ordinary biblical heroes who did extraordinary things for God... because he asked them to. Things that disrupted their lives, split apart their families, marred their reputations, sent them to strange lands, changed the trajectory of rising careers, and landed them in prison. They answered yes to a life of disruption, detours, loneliness, and poverty. All for an abundant life with him.

What? A life of abundance? But didn't you just say disruption, loneliness, broken families, ruined careers?

Yes, I did. The call to follow God without conditions, clauses, or caveats sometimes includes giving up the very things on which we are trying to build our lives. And sometimes they last for a season of growth and other times, such as in Paul's case, they last an entire lifetime.

But the reality is, disruption is always difficult no matter what. In our quest to build the perfect family, the perfect life, the perfect job, and the perfect community of friends, God often interrupts our plans. And when that happens, life can get painful and downright scary. The unknown can be frightening. The good news is God is not unknown; he is not inconsistent. God reveals Himself to us in his Word, the Holy Bible. His actions, however, can be unpredictable. After all, who can know the mind of God and predict how he will carry out his plan? (Job 36:23-26).

The willingness to say yes to God's disruption starts with a heart that seeks, above all, to say *yes* to God's call. We will see stories of people who answered God without hesitation, and some who thought about it for a while. In all these stories you will see a reflection of your own heart's story. It is my hope that you will be inspired to action, because inspiration without stepping out in faith will fade. It will make us feel good, for sure, but it won't change our lives. When we say yes to God and step out believing that he's got us, that is when our life will be never be the same.

ABOUT THIS BOOK

This book is meant to transform your life. It's more about implementing change than gathering information. This short, six-week study can either be done in a group or alone. If you are leading a group, there are some guidelines for leaders and resources in appendix 1 at the back of the book.

Each chapter includes three sections: Journal Points, Digging Deeper and Action Points. The **Journal Points** are like a highlighter. They are where to stop and write a response to something you are reading. I recommend you use a personal journal to accompany your study. Using a journal allows you to write as much or as little as you please. Take your time and really think through each Journal Point before you write.

At the end of each chapter is a **Digging Deeper** section with optional extended study suggestions. These are followed by **Action Points**, which help you apply what you're learning with journal writing and other resources.

One of the biggest drawbacks of Bible studies is that after the six to ten weeks, most people lay aside what they've done and move on to the next project, forgetting what they've learned. At the end of this study you'll find thirty days of devotionals designed to drive the content deeper into your life. I recommend doing one a day. After the thirty days you'll have a much richer relationship with the material in the book and be more likely to be on the journey to a transformed life.

To go even deeper, I invite you to connect with a wonderful community on our Women Finishing Well Facebook page. Just search Facebook for Women Finishing Well or join at our website womenfinishingwell.com. You can subscribe to our podcast and mailing list there as well. We love to give away stuff, so I recommend you subscribe to the newsletter on our website.

If you haven't read our first Bible study titled *Women Finishing Well*, you can find your copy on Amazon. That study will help you build a legacy of faith that lasts for generations. It's all about embracing the life that God has given you—your everyday, ordinary life. And it's never too early or too late to start.

ABOUT THE AUTHOR

I am a lifelong teacher. I think I was teaching the neighbor kids when I was a toddler. In addition to leading Bible studies, I have taught at the high school, college, and Bible institute levels. My husband would say I am always teaching somebody something. I'm not sure if that's a compliment, but I'll take it.

I have an undergraduate degree in English from Montana State (#GoCats) and a graduate degree in athletics administration from Eastern Washington University (#GoEags) where I did my thesis work in crisis management. I also earned a certificate in pastoral leadership from the Yellowstone Valley Bible Institute in Billings, Montana.

I've taught high school English, coached high school volleyball, and worked in college athletics as a communications professional. Can I add antiques dealer and caterer to this list? I'm getting tired just writing all that. I am living a full life and have been exceedingly blessed despite all the disruptions and detours. My husband and I farm in northeast Montana near the Canadian border and escape to the Phoenix area during the cold winters. We have two grown daughters who are my best friends, a magnificent son-in-law, and one granddaughter, who is the cutest and smartest little granddaughter in the world—no lie. My mom was the biggest influence on my life as a writer and a mom. I miss her.

I love to speak at women's events, and you can get information about that here: **https://womenfinishingwell.com/speaking/** or email me at **chris@womenfinishingwell.com.** We also have an active community on Facebook called Women Finishing Well. My ministry co-founder Diane Bradley and I host a weekly podcast you can find on iTunes, Stitcher, or Spotify called Women Finishing Well. We'd love to connect with you.

SPECIAL THANKS

This book was a collaborative effort by many people. And here are a few that deserve a high five.

> Thank you, Diane Bradley, for being my partner in this ministry. Your encouragement, exhortation, and friendship mean the world to me. Every page of this book is influenced by you. God bless you, my friend and sister in Christ.

> Thank you, Rebecca, my talented author-daughter, who kept me on track and always offered her wisdom with generosity. I wish I had one smidgen of her talent.

> Three gifted professionals helped bring this book to life:
>
> - Geoffrey Stone, editor
>
> - Kristen Ingebretson, cover artist
>
> - Steve Kuhn, KUHN Design Group, interior design and typesetting

I am blessed to have access to such a talented group.

Chapter One

THE MISTAKEN IDENTITY
What Does The Abundant Life Really Look Like?

*"The thief comes only to steal and kill and destroy.
I came that they may have life and have it abundantly."*

JOHN 10:10 ESV

*"Consider it pure joy, my brothers and sisters, whenever you face
trials of many kinds, because you know that the testing of your
faith produces perseverance. Let perseverance finish its work so
that you may be mature and complete, not lacking anything."*

JAMES 1:2-4

I am a huge fan of the *Great British Baking Show*. I've seen every season at least twice. My favorite episode is the final challenge of season ten where three bakers each made a spread of baked delights that masqueraded as regular picnic fare. The winner produced mini breads that looked like ripe peaches, fig bars that looked like sausage rolls, and small lemon pound cakes covered with fondant that looked like hunks of cheese on a cheese board. Even the picnic basket was made of biscuit. It was a masterful illusion of mistaken identity.

Jesus said in John 10:10 that he had come to give *us* abundant life. Jesus, the Shepherd, was talking to his sheep. The interesting thing about this verse we quote all the time is that it's found in the middle of a contentious conversation Jesus was having with the Pharisees that began when he healed a blind man on the Sabbath. Jesus identified himself as the Good Shepherd his sheep will follow because they know his voice. The Pharisees were represented in the story as thieves and robbers who come to destroy the sheep (vv. 7-10). As a matter of fact, the first half of verse ten is rarely quoted with the second half: "the thief comes only to steal and kill and destroy." But we can't afford to separate the two thoughts in verse ten even though we don't like to talk about the steal, kill, and destroy stuff. When we do, we forget that there is a liar embedded on the other side of that truth: one who will destroy us.

A NICE LITTLE LIFE

So what is the danger that lies in verse ten? The danger is in forgetting that we have an enemy. A thief that is out to steal the abundant life Jesus was talking about and replace it with an illusion that *looks* like abundance. And how does the enemy do that? By misidentifying what the real abundant life looks like. The Greek word for life in this verse, *zoe*, means a comprehensive, spirit-filled, eternal God-given life as opposed to the life defined by works of the flesh the enemy wants us to buy into.

Today, the abundant life has morphed into a picture of a nice little life: a good job, a nice home, well-behaved kids, a supportive marriage, an enjoyable church family, and maybe a nice vacation once in a while. Too often we have mistaken the abundant life Jesus died to give us for a worldly illusion of comfort. We need a massive paradigm shift anchored in three words: no matter what. Author, worship leader, and self-professed hope dealer Carlos Whittaker puts it this way:

> Abundance has nothing to do with accumulating things and everything to do with accessing the King. When you start seeing John 10:10 through that lens, you realize that abundant life—life to the full—is available even in our darkest hours.[1]

Journal Point: Describe your version of "the abundant life." How do you feel when God disrupts your life by throwing a wrench in the works? Do you still consider that interruption part of the abundant life that Jesus promised? Why or why not?

THE TRUTH ABOUT DISRUPTION

God has a habit of throwing a wrench in our works. Throughout the Bible we see God asking people to do things that totally turned them upside down. Think of Moses minding his own business in the desert, trying to live a nice little life, and all of a sudden a burning bush shows up and changes the trajectory of his future. Think of Noah who was asked to build something he couldn't even fathom for a problem he had never seen—rain. Think of Joshua trying to figure out how to get to the promised land through the massive walls of Jericho and God giving him a plan that included only marching, trumpets, and shouting. God uses disruption to change our lives to do his work.

Disruption Has a Bad Rap

We are averse to disruption, trouble, suffering, and trials. I mean who wants trouble in their lives? Nobody, right? But the truth is we live in a fallen world and Christians are not exempt from trouble. Consider these Scriptures:

> "Those who suffer he delivers *in* their suffering; he speaks to them in their affliction." (Job 36:15)

> "Dear friends, do not be surprised at the fiery ordeal that has come on you to test you, as though something strange were happening to you. But rejoice inasmuch as you participate in the sufferings

of Christ, so that you may be overjoyed when his glory is revealed."
(1 Peter 4:12-13)

"Consider it pure joy, my brothers and sisters, whenever you face trials of many kinds, because you know that the testing of your faith
produces perseverance. Let perseverance finish its work so that you
may be mature and complete, not lacking anything." (James 1:2-4)

"Therefore do not worry about tomorrow, for tomorrow will worry
about itself. Each day has enough trouble of its own." (Matthew 6:34)

We need to start at square one: God uses trouble for our good (Romans
8:28). He sometimes brings disruption to grow and mature us, whether we like
it or not. We can hesitate, turn our back, stop in our tracks, or cry out in despair,
but God is still there holding on to us. More on that later.

Journal Point: Which of the four Scriptures above challenge
your belief about suffering the most? Why? What is your first
reaction to adversity?

It is important to remember that Peter told us we can suffer for doing wrong
(1 Peter 4:15). But for our purpose in this study we are not going to differentiate
between disruption caused by poor decisions or disruption straight from God's
hand for our growth. God uses them both for his purpose, which is to draw us
closer to him—where the abundant life is.

The other thing we need to get clear on is that disruption is not a punishment either. Remember Jesus already took the punishment for our sins, and

God will forgive us when we confess our sins. However, some actions have consequences, and we can't always escape those.

Journal Point: What is the difference between disruption caused by our sins and disruption that God brings to refine and grow us? Is there a time in your life you made a bad decision that resulted in a consequence you needed to walk through? How has God used that to bring you closer to him?

Age Is Not an Excuse

The older we get, the harder it is to face disruptions and detours with a willing heart. It is easy to buy into the lie that we deserve a hassle-free life in our later years. But this season has the potential to be the most exciting, the most abundant, and the most impactful season of any we have lived yet. Most of us have more time, more flexibility, more wisdom, more experience, and sometimes more resources than other generations to help further the kingdom of God. The enemy knows the baby boomer generation has the potential to be the biggest army for God in this present age. So the forces of evil will attack us with all the old standby lies: you're useless, nobody wants you, you've worked hard, it's your time to take it easy and coast. As guardians of the generations coming after us, we cannot be the generation that drops the baton of faith. We must guard our hearts. The truth is, disruptions are part of the abundant life journey at all ages. So be willing to put aside your preconceived notions about what the abundant life looks like at your age and get busy for God. Age is not an excuse; it is your platform.

> *Journal Point:* Do you ever find yourself using your age (either too young or too old) as an excuse to avoid disruptions in your life? What messages are playing in your head when that happens?

THE SECRET PATH

Life's disruptions are like a secret path that everybody knows about, but nobody wants to look for. Even though the Bible is filled with signs that show us the way, few of us are really interested in a life filled with challenges. And when we do get a whiff of disruption, we tend to recoil instead of quicken our pace on the path. Again, who really wants a life filled with trouble?

Grappling with the Great Paradox

All my Christian life I've had trouble with James 1:2-4. I've yet to meet anyone that gets giddy at the thought of facing "trials of many kinds." So why does that verse say, "consider it pure joy my brothers and sisters, whenever you face trials of many kinds." I've studied the original language. I've looked at different Bible versions to see if the meaning is any different. I mean, surely The Message must have something more palatable. Nope, no relief there. The Message says, "consider it a sheer gift." The New Living Translations says, "consider it a great opportunity of great joy."

For years I bristled at these verses thinking they were asking me to "grit your teeth and force yourself to be joyful." After all, it could be worse, right? But what I didn't get until relatively recently is that these verses represent one of the great paradoxes of the Bible. According to Merriam-Webster, a paradox is "a statement that is seemingly contradictory or opposed to common sense and yet is perhaps true." In my studies of biblical paradoxes I've found that God's Word is loaded with these apparent contradictions. The first will be last; the poor will inherit the earth; when I am weak, then I am strong; we gain through losing; we live by dying. Friend, God isn't worried that we don't *get* it. But in order to move into abundant life, we have to *believe* it.

> **Journal Point:** What are some of the biblical paradoxes you find the hardest to believe? Why? To get started, check out the Sermon on the Mount in Matthew 5:3-16.

GOD'S GOAL IN DISRUPTING OUR LIFES

Let's go back to James 1. This is where we find God's goal for testing in our lives:

> because you know that the testing of your faith produces perseverance. Let perseverance finish its work so that you may be mature and complete, *not lacking anything.* (vv. 3-4, emphasis mine)

Not lacking *anything.* Wouldn't you say that's a pretty good definition of abundance? Next comes the million-dollar question: what does the word *anything* mean? Is that a winning lottery ticket? A life without sickness? A marriage that stays together for life? Remember the Greek word *zoe?* That is the word Jesus used to describe an abundant life in John 10:10, and it means a full spiritual life, a life of full access to the eternal God. I just heard a virtual collective sigh.

Still not convinced that a *zoe* life is better than a life with all the benefits of the world? Let's take a look at Galatians 5:19-21. Here is Paul's list of the benefits of a life lived in the flesh: sexual immorality, impurity, lustful pleasures, idolatry, sorcery, hostility, quarreling, jealousy, outbursts of anger, selfish ambition, dissension, division, envy, drunkenness, wild parties, and other sins like these. A life in the flesh is a life filled with caveats, contradictions, and conflicts with God to get what you want. Contrast that with a life of love, joy, peace, patience, kindness, goodness, faithfulness, gentleness, and self-control in verses 22-23. A life that is "in step with the Spirit" (v. 25) is a life where "no matter what" is your motto. And if you need more convincing, read Ephesians 1:3-14. Personalize it in your journal. Say it out loud every day. Top that off with Psalm 139 and a big helping of Matthew 28:20 and Hebrews 13:5-6.

That is the promise of your abundant life. That is what we get when we embrace disruption.

> *Journal Point:* Read Galatians 5:22-26, Ephesians 1:3-14, Psalm 139: 1-6, 13-18, Matthew 28:20, and Hebrews 13:5-6. Make a list of the promises of God that stand out to you. Write them in the first person (I, my, me, mine). I challenge you to make it a priority to declare them out loud every day. Of all the habits you can pick up in this study, this one is at the top of the list.

How to Clear the Path

The path to abundant life is not so much a secret path as it is an overgrown path. It's been neglected with creeping vines of fear, thick branches of past failures and shame, overgrown weeds of biblical misunderstanding, ruts of unbelief and dangling disappointments of life events. The way to abundant life starts with clearing away the lies of what the Christian life is like in our imagination and start making level paths for our feet with the truth.

We do not create an abundant life for ourselves. We experience it by embracing the life God has given us. The abundant life is not a formula; it is a process of following where God leads, clearing out the underbrush one section at a time. When we reveal the bedrock footpath, we can see that our plans are not the best; God's plans are (Proverbs 16:9). The abundant life is walking in the truth of Ephesians 2:10: "For [I am] God's handiwork, created in Christ Jesus to do good works, which God prepared in advance for [me] to do."

No matter what. Are you ready to answer God's call to disruption in your life today?

Journal Point: Why do you think we don't want to embrace disruption no matter what? What are some of the common excuses we use?

Journal Point: What are some of the roadblocks and disruptions in your life right now? How are you handling them? What part of God's disruptions is the most uncomfortable for you right now? The most comfortable?

Digging Deeper:

For an increased understanding of the material in this chapter, I recommend you study the following passages using the SOAP method found in appendix 2 on page 145. Use your journal to record your studies.

- James 1:2-4
- John 10: 1-18
- Matthew 6:25-34
- Ephesians 1:3-14

Action Point:

1. Declaring and praying the Word of God is an important habit to develop in our search for the abundant life. One thing I've found that really turbo boosts the power of prayer is to write it out in a conversational, first-person form. Keep some index cards handy for writing out verses you want to memorize or declare daily.

2. Start this essential habit by writing out Ephesians 1:3-14 in a first person abbreviated style. You can either copy mine below or make up your own to match the version of the Bible you like. I have this in a pile of Bible verses I try and say every morning. Sometimes I take them on my morning walk. Keep it handy and start a habit of praying it to God every day.

3. Here is an example of a personalized version of Ephesians 1:3-14:

4. *I am* blessed in the heavenly realms with every spiritual blessing in Christ. *I am* chosen to be holy and blameless in Your sight. *I am* your adopted child. You've redeemed *me* from death; you've lavished your grace on *me*. You've made known the mystery of your will *to me. I am* marked with Your sealed Holy Spirit guaranteeing *my* inheritance. Thank you God that you have forgiven all *my* sins."

5. Start the habit today before you go on to chapter two. Personalize your version of Ephesians 1:3-14.

Chapter Two

THE MARY ANSWER

*"You did not choose me, but I chose you and appointed you so that
you might go and bear fruit—fruit that will last—and so that
whatever you ask in my name the Father will give you."*

JOHN 15:16

*He has saved us and called us to a holy life—not because of anything
we have done but because of his own purpose and grace. This grace
was given us in Christ Jesus before the beginning of time.*

2 TIMOTHY 1:9

*"So here's what I want you to do, God helping you: Take your everyday,
ordinary life—your sleeping, eating, going-to-work, and walking-
around life—and place it before God as an offering. Embracing
what God does for you is the best things you can do for him."*

ROMANS 12:1 MSG

When our youngest daughter got engaged, she set out to plan her dream wedding. That's just who she is. She loves to plan events that make people happy. Whether it's a gourmet s'mores party on the fourth of July or an elaborate online baby shower for a college friend, she's on it and good at it.

Every detail of her wedding was designed to make everyone happy. From Jane Austen-themed table names (to which people were carefully assigned depending on the book) to a multiple-course, small-plate buffet that included a dessert table featuring traditional family favorites from both sides. Every detail was planned to reflect the love the bride and groom had for each other and for everyone there. We spent weeks filling custom printed cloth bags with gourmet cookies, maps, tickets to local attractions in San Diego, and a detailed calendar of all the weekend events for the wedding party and family members. Although the wedding took us over a year to plan, the seeds of that celebration were planted in my daughter's heart many years earlier.

THE SET-UP: A NICE LITTLE LIFE

In many cultures, weddings are a shared celebration of a new beginning. In the Jewish tradition of Jesus' time, marriages were usually arranged by parents. The groom's parents would choose a bride for their son. A one-year period of betrothal followed as the families got ready for the celebration and decided on a dowry for the bride's family. The actual wedding took place over a five- to seven-day period, which included much celebrating and ritual. Usually an entire village would gather for a wedding. I imagine that a young Jewish girl might have spent some time daydreaming about the who, when, and where of this exciting beginning of a new life.

I imagine Mary spent some time daydreaming about her new life. History records that both Mary and Joseph were from traditional Jewish families. Joseph's family was in the bloodline of King David. Her parents were probably ecstatic when the match was made. Mary set her heart on a wonderful life: establishing a household, being a good mom, and growing old with a man who lovingly devoted himself to his bride. No visions of grandeur. Just a pleasant, ordinary life for two ordinary people. Never in a million years did she expect a divine wedding planner named Gabriel to show up and disrupt her nice little life.

Journal Point: Can you identify with the desire to have a "nice little life"? What does that look like for you? How would you feel if God disrupted it?

THE DIVINE INVITATION

Sometime during the one-year waiting period of Mary's engagement, God sent the angel Gabriel to her home in Nazareth with a series of three massive disruptions.

The First Disruption: "Greetings you who are highly favored! The Lord is with you" (Luke 1:28). The first words Gabriel spoke to Mary are key to understanding the way God brings disruption into all our lives. Now this is no ordinary greeting. The Greek greeting in that verse literally means "glad for grace." It is a greeting often used for royalty. He then follows that up with a word that occurs only one time in the New Testament and is translated as "highly favored one of grace." It is a cognate or a derivative of a word in Ephesians 1:6 that Paul uses to describes the grace God gives us. Gabriel is letting Mary know that she has been chosen by God for something she could have never dreamed of—something way beyond her expectations of a nice little life with Joseph.

It always struck me as odd that she wasn't disturbed by the angel's appearance but just his greeting. Luke tells us that "Mary was greatly troubled at his words and wondered what kind of greeting this might be" (v. 29). Right away, the angel assures her all is well: "Do not be afraid, Mary" (v. 30). Notice he used her name. It's amazing how hearing our name can get our attention and disarm our fears when we are unsettled. Just to assure her he repeats, "you have found favor with God." She did hear him right the first time. She was highly favored.

Mary needed to understand the greeting was favorable, something she could rejoice in. She needed to understand hers was a mission from God that no other woman in history had received or would ever receive again. The statement indicated she was given a great honor. God showed Mary the truth of her calling before he showed her the logistics.

God does this with us as well. Grace always precedes the task. Even though this declaration from the angel was one that should have brought her confidence and blessing, she was greatly troubled. Sometimes we fear disruption because we fear the unknown. But God is just asking us to embrace everything *he* believes about us. We need to guard our hearts against the lies lurking in the dark parts of our hearts. Lies that we are not good enough, that the promises of God don't apply to us, or that we don't completely trust that God has our best interests at heart.

The Second Disruption: "You will conceive and give birth to a son, and you are to call him Jesus. He will be great and will be called the Son of the Most

High. The Lord will give him the throne of his father David and he will reign over Jacob's descendants forever; his kingdom will never end" (Luke 1:31-33). With this statement, the light bulb starts to go off. Mary isn't married yet, right? So she asks the obvious question: "How will this be since I am a virgin?" (v. 34). What comes next changed her life forever.

The Third Disruption: "The angel answered, 'The Holy Spirit will come on you, and the power of the Most High will overshadow you. So the holy one to be born will be called the Son of God' " (v. 35). The other shoe just dropped.

Up until that moment giving birth to a special man of God might have felt like a blessing, something wonderful to look forward to, something to bring her union with Joseph favor among her family and friends. Delightful. But the angel's next thirty-one words shattered that whole dreamy picture. The euphoric anticipation of favor and blessing just vanished in an instant.

> *Journal Point:* Looking back at each one of these three disruptions, which would be the hardest for you to accept? Why? Can you put yourself in Mary's position and imagine what she might be feeling at this point?

THE MARY ANSWER

Many of us would likely have thought "this is not fair" or "what have I done to deserve this?" The one thing that God's disruptions prove to us is that life is *not* fair. The Bible *never* teaches that disruptions are punishment for something we did or didn't do. It does teach that disruptions are proving grounds (see James 1:2-4).

Everything God does is just. "His works are perfect, and all his ways are just. A faithful God who does no wrong, upright and just is he" (Deuteronomy 32:4).

"This isn't fair" might have been David's motto as a young man. It took twenty years from the time he was anointed as king to the time he actually became king. And four times in the book of 1 Samuel, during the time of his proving ground, David asked the question, "what have I done now?" (17:29, 20:1, 26:18, 29:7). Each roadblock, each setback was frustrating. But that shepherd boy had a lot of learning to do before he ascended to the throne of the king. The degree to which you can embrace "this isn't fair" and move on is the degree to which you will fulfill God's purpose for your life.

> *Journal Point:* Can you think of a time in your life when a disruption seemed unfair? How did you react? Did you try and line up the disruption with God's Word or with something you had done? What did you learn?

Mary's answer to the angel's proclamation showed she was ready to embrace disruption. She wasn't holding anything back. She had no more questions, no doubts. Her answer was a short but powerful, "I am the Lord's servant. May your word to me be fulfilled" (Luke 1:38). May God help us respond to life's disruptions with the same simple and confident faith.

One Answer to Rule Them All

Throughout this study we are going to look at several "answers" to God's disruptions in light of Mary's unconditional answer. To understand how her unfettered answer becomes our ultimate example, it's important to see how her answer ushered in a different life than the one she likely dreamed of having—a nice little life.

As a woman embedded in the patriarchal Jewish culture of royalty, Mary was in line to marry a man from the royal family of Judaism. In Genesis 49:8-12, Jacob pronounced a blessing on Judah by announcing his descendants would be rulers over the nation of Israel. David was from the tribe of Judah, and Mary's betrothed, Joseph, was a descendant of David. Joseph's family was what we might call middle class but being related to David was still a big deal. Why is this important? Because when it got out among the Jewish elite that Mary was pregnant without being married, she knew there would be gossiping and whispering. Mary knew there would be consequences when she said yes. She didn't have to see the future. She knew there would be a cost. As a matter of fact, it's a good thing she didn't see it, because this is just a sample of what she would have seen:

- A long pregnant trek on a donkey that ended with a rustic birth in a stable.

- A quick getaway to Egypt to escape a threat of death, and her first three years as a mom spent away from the safety and tutoring of her extended family.

- The ruling Jewish elite claiming her oldest son had a demon and was a blasphemer.

- Sitting at the foot of the cross and watching her grown son die the most agonizing death possible despite doing nothing wrong.

This kind of unwavering devotion to God's call emanates from the heartfelt belief that God is for us and not against us. Mary embraced the kind of disruption we talked about in chapter one. God's disruptions mature and complete us so that we are *not lacking anything* (James 1:4). This is the abundant life that Jesus died to bring us.

Journal Point: Write out a prayer asking God to show you what might be standing in the way of you giving him an unhindered yes when he calls. Don't be discouraged if you don't feel you hear anything right away. Listening is a skill that takes some practice. Remember James 1:4: "Let perseverance finish its work so that you may be mature and complete, not lacking anything." Hang in there.

THOUGHTS FOR OUR JOURNEY

Learning to respond to life with the Mary Answer takes time. It is a journey. Most of us don't get there the first time we are faced with a decision to respond to God's leading. And that is because we are travelers on a road. Life isn't Final Jeopardy where one right answer gives us the win. Life is more like Chutes and Ladders, full of disruptions and detours. But we do see from Mary's life that there were things she did to position herself for victory.

The Friends and Family Plan

After Mary was visited by the angel, she went to see her relative Elizabeth. Mary probably knew Elizabeth's story of barrenness (Luke 1:7) and was inspired to go visit after the angel mentioned she was pregnant. Can we assume at this point that Mary was feeling a little confused? Maybe lonely? Worried about how people were going to react to the news of her pregnancy? Whatever trepidation she was experiencing melted away when she saw Elizabeth:

> The baby leaped in her womb, and Elizabeth was filled with the Holy Spirit. In a loud voice she exclaimed: "Blessed are you among

women, and blessed is the child you will bear! But why am I so favored, that the mother of my Lord should come to me? As soon as the sound of your greeting reached my ears, the baby in my womb leaped for joy. Blessed is she who has believed that the Lord would fulfill his promises to her!" (Luke 1:41-45)

Talk about a confidence boost! How validating this must have been for Mary. Elizabeth's inspiring greeting gave her the confidence to break out in song in Luke 1:46-55. She was able to let go in a safe environment and praise God with every fiber of her being. What a comradery of God's miracles they became. What a testimony to the power of friends in the faith. We all need friends like Elizabeth in our life who support and encourage our calling.

When I decided to quit a successful book marketing business in 2019 to pursue a call God had given me years earlier, many of my friends were puzzled. My business associates thought I was nuts. Who works their way up the ladder and then quits when they are almost at the top? But I knew it was time. And my new ministry co-pilot confirmed that calling, so off we went despite the naysayers. Having an Elizabeth by my side made all the difference.

You need to find your Elizabeth no matter what you're facing—whether it's a decision to change jobs, to stay at home, to become a writer or speaker, to volunteer in a prison, to travel as a part-time missionary, to be a daycare provider for your grandkids, or to head up your neighborhood watch. Maybe it's a decision to lead a Bible study, start a morning time with God, or temper your social media or TV watching. What is it God is calling you to do? If you really want to hear, he'll let you know. And he'll help you find your Elizabeths.

Journal Point: Is there something you feel God has been asking you or leading you to do? To give up? To change? Do you have women around you who support you? Write a prayer for God to bring you some Elizabeths if you don't have any. If you do have sister friends around you, what is it about them that gives you confidence?

Learn How to Play Chutes and Ladders

When I was first married there were a number of older Christian women in my church I admired. One in particular was a beautiful prayer warrior who always had an encouraging word for everyone. She knew her Bible inside out, was humble, and always raised her hand when something needed to be done. I wanted to be like Blanche. I prayed to be like Blanche. I was so impatient to get there that I prayed to travel on a straight line from where I was to right where she was. And be there tomorrow.

One night as I was tossing and turning, pondering how I could be more like Blanche, God showed me a picture. It wasn't projected on the wall like the handwriting at Belshazzar's banquet in the book of Daniel, but I could see it clearly in my mind. I saw a life-sized gameboard of Chutes and Ladders—remember I had small children at the time—and I was in a car speeding like mad trying to get to the top of the board. But the gameboard was full of curves and stops and detours. Sometimes I landed at the bottom of a ladder where I scooted up to another road—car and all—only to land on a chute and tumble downward back to an earlier location. It was frustrating, and I never remember getting to the top. But I do remember the picture God was trying to show me: life rarely turns out like we think it will, and it rarely progresses as fast as we hope. Remember all those things Mary was going to face in her life that the angel didn't tell her about? We are called to trust, not to plan the quickest route. What you're going through right now is preparation for *where* you're going. Submit yourself to the process. Life doesn't always go the way we expect. And that's a good thing.

Journal Point: Is there something in your life right now that feels like a constant downward chute on the game board of life? Do you feel like you just can't seem to make any forward progress? Write about the experience and ask God to help you understand how to submit yourself to the process.

MARY'S EPILOGUE

We don't see Mary much in the rest of the New Testament. She is mentioned when they present Jesus at the temple as a baby, when they make an annual trek to the temple and accidentally leave him behind, when she asked him to turn water into wine, and we see her at the foot of the cross watching his death. One other place we see her is in Acts 1:12-14, right after Jesus' death, as one of the original prayer warriors in the early days of the Jerusalem church. Perseverance was finishing its work (James 1:2-4). Mary's life had not been easy, but she stayed the course; she ran the marathon. She got to the top of the gameboard.

Don't ever doubt what God has called you to do. You may be asked to live much of your life in obscurity, or on a stage where all your flaws are visible. Whatever he calls you to do, make sure you follow in Mary's footsteps and answer, "I am the Lord's servant. May everything you have said about me come true."

Digging Deeper:

For an increased understanding of the material in this chapter, I recommend you study the following passages using the SOAP method found in appendix 2 on page 145. Use your journal to record your studies.

- John 15:7-17
- Romans 12:1-2 (from The Message version)
- Luke 1:26-56
- David's four dilemmas (1 Samuel 17:29, 20:1, 26:18, 29:7)

Action Points:

1. If you don't have the YouVersion Bible app on your smartphone. you can download it for free at *https://bible.com/app*. There are versions for all types of devices and over 200 versions of the Bible on this handy app. Once you navigate your way around, you'll be using it all the time—I promise. If you don't have a smartphone, you can access the app directly on your computer at https://www.bible.com/.

2. Are you struggling to respond positively to something you know God has called you to do? Do a word search on the YouVersion Bible app for plans on trust. If you like to do your own digging, you can use a concordance or topical Bible on the biblestudytools.com site and do a word study on *trust*.

Chapter Three

NO IFS, ANDS, OR BUTS— THEY WERE ALL-IN

"Now faith is confidence in what we hope for and assurance about what we do not see. This is what the ancients were commended for."

HEBREWS 11:1-2

"Whoever wants to be my disciple must deny themselves and take up their cross and follow me. For whoever wants to save his life will lose it, but he who loses his life for me will find it."

MATTHEW 16:24-25

"So we fix our eyes not on what is seen, but on what is unseen, since what is seen is temporary, but what is unseen is eternal."

2 CORINTHIANS 4:18

In the movie *Indiana Jones and the Last Crusade* the hero has to navigate a series of cryptic challenges to retrieve a challis that has supernatural powers to heal his father's fatal gunshot wound. The answers to each challenge are carefully detailed in his father's diary. He has to trust in his father's diary or face certain death. On the last challenge, Indiana Jones is faced with a large chasm of sheer rock that he must cross to grab the cup and save his father. What he saw was impossible. Until he realized that he had to believe in what he couldn't see. The feat required a leap of faith. As he closed his eyes and stepped out, his foot landed solidly on a narrow stone bridge that had blended perfectly into the sheer rock wall on the other side.[1] He had confidence in what he couldn't see.

WHAT THE ANCIENTS
WERE COMMENDED FOR

Hebrews 11 is a Who's Who of faith. We are very familiar with some of the people mentioned and some we may be only vaguely familiar to us. But everyone mentioned in that passage accomplished amazing things on God's behalf by faith. These Old Testament heroes and heroines had one thing in common: they all had confidence in what they hoped for and assurance of that which they couldn't see (Hebrews 11:1).

The all-star list describes leaps of faith by Abel, Noah, Abraham, Isaac, Jacob, Joseph, and Moses. Legacy-worthy groups are included: the people who passed through the Red Sea and those who marched around the walls of Jericho until it fell with just a shout. The writer then mentions some legends of faith (David, Gideon, and others) and ends with a list of hardships that many unnamed heroes of faith endured (vv. 35-38).

If this list had included New Testament heroes, Mary would no doubt be listed. As we start this chapter on people in the Bible who gave an unreserved yes to God's invitation, let's remember that Mary's answer to God's invitation was not a biblical outlier; it was not a one-off. It was the extraordinary standard that God is calling us all to. She showed us how the abundant life begins with a confidence in what we can't see and an assurance of what we hope for. It is what the ancients were commended for (Hebrews 11:2).

The people we will look at in this chapter had real lives just like us. They are a motley crew: a bullied childless wife, a young woman who gave up the safety of homeland and family to become an immigrant, and a man who left a lucrative political career to follow God into a prison cell. This is us. And they are part of that great cloud of witnesses (Hebrews 12:1-3) cheering us on down here, hoping we will answer God's divine invitation to step into the unknown just as they did. But remember, they see clearly something that is off in the distance for us: There is joy on the other side of every disruption and detour that comes in our path.

Journal Point: Which of the heroes of faith listed in Hebrews 11 is the biggest inspiration to you? Why?

HANNAH: THE ANNUAL DISAPPOINTMENT

As a kid, every summer we took a vacation to my grandparents' lake house in northern Wisconsin. I would start dreaming about that trip on January 1, and I would reminisce about the fun times for months after it was over in August. It was the highlight of every year growing up. In 1 Samuel 1:1-8 we see an annual family trip that was anything but enjoyable. In fact, Hannah's annual family trek to the house of worship in Shiloh was an exercise in torture. It was a disruption she dreaded year after year (v. 3).

Hannah was one of two wives of Elkanah, a Levite who lived about twelve miles from Shiloh, the nearest house of worship. Elkanah's other wife, Peninnah, had a bunch of kids but Hannah had none. Every year Elkanah marched this family entourage to Shiloh to make a sacrifice to God, and every year Peninnah bullied Hannah about being barren until she was so distraught she couldn't eat. Elkanah tried to encourage Hannah, but reminding her that he could mean more to her than ten sons did not ease her pain. Duh.

THE SET-UP: HANNAH'S PROMISE

After supper one evening, Hannah stood up and began to pray in deep anguish, and weeping bitterly, she made a pact with God: "If you give me a son, I'll give him back to you." The priest Eli noticed her anguish, and he initially mistook it for drunkenness. Oftentimes our disruptions and detours look like something totally different to the people around us. They may mistake our motives. But they don't see what's confronting us; they don't see our hearts. Sometimes our disruptions can even be misinterpreted as sin.

Our disruptions will run up against opposition. At a time when we are trying to push through to God, we may experience persecution instead of encouragement. This is one of the enemy's specialties. He doesn't care how it happens; he just wants your disruption to look like a roadblock. He knows what's on the other side if we keep moving ahead with God. And he'll use the people around you—even those who love you—to discourage you. Remember Job's three friends—more like Job's three frenemies? Jesus reminds us that mistreatment can be a good thing:

> God blesses you when people mock you and persecute you and lie about you and say all sorts of evil things against you because you are my followers. Be happy about it! Be very glad! For a great reward awaits you in heaven. And remember, the ancient prophets were persecuted in the same way. (Matthew 5:11-12 NLT)

Journal Point: Has there ever been a time in your life when the people around you questioned or even criticized a decision you made to follow God into trouble? A time when you were expecting support from a friend or loved one and instead got pushback? Describe how you worked through that.

THE DIVINE INVITATION

Hannah's divine invitation came in the form of a promise she made to God in prayer (1 Samuel 1:9). Some speculate that Hannah's promise was made in a moment of emotion fueled by anguish. But I think Hannah knew exactly what she was doing and where to take her sorrow. First, Hannah was a praying woman. Although appearing only briefly in the Old Testament, over half the time we see her, she is praying. In her prayer of praise (1 Samuel 2:1-10) we see that Hannah trusted God to do whatever was best, and she was confident that God's favor was not earned but came by his grace.

HANNAH'S ANSWER: THE SACRIFICE

Hannah answered God's invitation by giving away the one thing she had been seeking for years—the one thing that would have put an end to all the bullying and whispers and tears. And that one faithful act of giving Samuel up was rewarded greatly. She ended up having six more children and her place in the family was restored: "Now I have an answer for my enemies. . . The childless woman now has seven children, and the woman with many children wastes away" (1 Samuel 2:1, 5).

Journal Point: Read Hannah's prayer in 1 Samuel 2:1-10. What specific situations is Hannah describing here that she experienced during her barren years? According to verses 9-10 what will happen to those who oppose God's faithful?

Journal Point: What were some of the risks Hannah took in making a promise to God to give up her firstborn son to his service? Have you ever made a promise to God as a declaration of faith? What did that look like?

RUTH: LOSING YOUR LIFE TO FIND IT

The precept of self-sacrifice is predominant in the gospels. But really, how easy is giving up everything we want so God can have his way? The concept of dying to self is often associated with living a life of poverty or isolation. It isn't very appealing. Yet, we know God wants us to hand the reins over to him, but we don't really want to give up *everything*.

Jesus talks about this specific lifestyle twice in Matthew's gospel alone. When he first sent out the twelve, he told the disciples what would be required of them: "Whoever does not take up their cross and follow me is not worthy of me. Whoever finds their life will lose it, and whoever loses their life for my sake will find it" (Matthew 10:38-39). Jesus reminded them of this when he was speaking with them about his upcoming death (Matthew 16:24-25). There is a secret here that the disciples were missing. When you give up everything, you don't lose anything important. As a matter of fact, when you lose your life, you'll find the abundant life God has for you, a life that is "superabundantly more than all we dare ask or think" (Ephesians 3:20 AMP).

Mary knew that secret deep in her heart. So did Hannah. And so did Ruth.

THE SET-UP: RUTH'S FAMILY MATTERS

Ruth had her own version of sorrow. Like Hannah's, it was a family affair. A Jewish family with two sons escaped a drought in their homeland of Israel and fled to neighboring Moab, a Gentile nation. After Ruth married one of the sons, all the men in her new family died within ten years, including her husband. When the drought in Israel was over, Naomi wanted to return to her family there. She told her daughters-in-law to return to their fathers' houses. Orpah returned, but Ruth insisted on coming with Naomi, which led to a divine invitation.

THE DIVINE INVITATION

Maybe Ruth just liked Naomi and preferred living with her over her own family. Maybe Ruth didn't know that hidden in this request from her mother-in-law was a divine invitation from God to abundant life—an abundant life that involved living as an immigrant in a strange land. But her soft heart of servanthood was being prepared even as they began their journey to Israel. After they started out, Naomi asked both daughters-in-law to go back to their family homes—twice. After two tries, Naomi could not get Ruth to leave. God was at work in Ruth's persistence.

RUTH'S ANSWER

What Ruth said next to Naomi set the course of both their lives on a path to God's abundant provision:

> "Don't urge me to leave you and turn back from you. Where you go I will go, and where you stay I will stay. Your people will be my people and your God my God. Where you die, I will die, and there I will be buried. May the LORD deal with me, be it ever so severely, if even death separates you and me."

When Naomi realized that Ruth was determined to go with her, she stopped urging her. (Ruth 1:16-18)

Ruth made a declaration that Naomi's God (Elohim) would now be her God. But she likely didn't realize that answering that invitation would result in the restoration of the family she and Naomi had started in Moab and much more. God's response to her answer exceeded Ruth and Naomi's expectations—abundantly above all they could dare ask or think. And Ruth's answer had one far reaching consequence that changed the course of mankind. When Boaz, a relative of Naomi's husband, married Ruth, she gave birth to a son named Obed. Obed was the grandfather of King David. And according to Matthew's genealogy, Jesus was a son of David (Matthew 1:1). You never know what's on the other side of the disruption in your life.

Journal Point: Put yourself in Ruth's place. Would you leave your homeland and travel to a foreign country that is known for being hostile to your people? Would you stay or would you go? Why?

Journal Point: Have you ever had a situation in your life where you lost something you treasured, and God restored that back to you over and above what you expected? Describe that experience.

PAUL:
DOING A SPIRITUAL 180

William Wilberforce grew up in a wealthy family in late eighteenth century England. His Cambridge education and family position set him up to enter parliament at twenty-four years of age. On Easter 1786 young William "experienced a spiritual rebirth" which left him in a quandary.[2] Wilberforce's new faith was evangelical—meaning that he believed his faith needed to be acted upon---a belief that the wealthy religious of his time looked down upon. They believed in a sovereign God and the church, but they didn't really want that belief to interfere with their lives. As Wilberforce's political career rose, it started to clash with his faith. He contemplated leaving politics to take up the unpopular struggle to abolish the slave trade.

Close friends, including the prime minister, William Pitt, convinced him that he could serve both God and the parliament. This ushered in an adult life dedicated to seeing slavery eradicated from the British Empire—something that was accomplished just three days before his death in 1833.

THE SET-UP:
RISING TO THE TOP

The apostle Paul's early life was similar to William Wilberforce's life. Paul's pedigree and education set him up for an early rise in the Jewish ruling culture. We don't have any evidence that Paul came from a wealthy family, but we know he worked diligently to be what today we might call a self-made man (Philippians 3:4-6).

We are first introduced to Paul by his Jewish name Saul. Early in his career, we find him overseeing the imprisonment and death of Christian Jews. As the angry mob dragged Stephen outside of town to stone him for his profession of faith, "the witnesses laid their coats at the feet of a young man named Saul" (Acts 7:58). Amazingly, God used this very event to grow the church as believers were scattered throughout the region in fear (Acts. 11:19). God was setting Paul up.

Journal Point: Are there events in your life (before God) that set you up to be saved? Can you point to specific events since your salvation that led you to a deeper relationship with God? Journal some of these stories and ask God to help you remember them. Thank him for leading you to where you are right now. Writing and remembering them will give you confidence to share them with others.

THE DIVINE INVITATION

As his power grew, Paul started stepping up his murderous game. He asked the high priest in Jerusalem for permission to go to Damascus, so he could drag Christian Jews back to Jerusalem as prisoners (Acts 9:1-2). But God decided to give Paul a couple detours that ended up being his divine invitation.

The first detour came as a blinding light (literally) on the road to Damascus followed by an encounter with Jesus. After Saul was struck blind, Jesus identified himself and told him to go to Damascus and wait for instructions. Through the prayer of a local believer named Ananias, Paul received his sight and his marching orders (Acts 9:17-19).

PAUL'S ANSWER

The next detour is the pièce de résistance in Paul's conversion. He went directly to the synagogues in Damascus, as he had originally planned, not to arrest the disciples but to preach about Jesus *as* a disciple. Wow! A definite spiritual one eighty. We don't have any evidence that reveals a conversation Paul had with God about his future at this time. But true to his life's story of being a doer, Paul poured his whole being into his work without thinking of the repercussions. As he wrote in Philippians 1:21, "For to me, living means living for Christ, and dying is even better." Paul's answer to God was an unreserved, all-in, no-excuses, stepping-out-in-faith commitment.

Paul got so powerful in the Holy Spirit that the Jews in Damascus plotted to put him to death. After the threat made its way to the Damascus believers, they smuggled Paul out of the city, saving the very man who had promised to drag them off to prison.

Journal Point: Has God ever asked you to do something that filled you with fear? What was that process like? How did you overcome your fear?

Journal Point: What are some of the "excuses" you have made in the past to step out in your faith.

THOUGHTS FOR OUR JOURNEY

Each person in this chapter had a divine invitation that disrupted their life. But no one put this in perspective better than Paul. If we want to go all-in with God, we have to give up our life. Hannah gave up Samuel—the only thing she ever wanted in life. Ruth gave up her homeland and her family to become a widowed immigrant to serve her mother-in-law. And Paul gave up a powerful life that would be hard to walk away from:

> If someone else thinks they have reasons to put confidence in the flesh, I have more: circumcised on the eighth day, of the people of Israel, of the tribe of Benjamin, a Hebrew of Hebrews; in regard to the law, a Pharisee; as for zeal, persecuting the church; as for righteousness based on the law, faultless. (Philippians 3:4-6)

All of these people gave up their lives, not because they were forced to but because deep in their hearts they knew it was the path to abundant life with God. They made a major paradigm shift. Their lives went from being all about themselves to being all about God. And God is calling us to this shift as well. Jesus said if we want to save our life, we will lose it. But if we lose our life for him, we will find it (Matthew 16:25, Mark 8:35, Luke 9:24). Losing your life isn't about giving up everything you have and moving to Africa, but it might be. Paul reminds us it's not about *what* we will lose; it's about the *why*:

> But whatever were gains to me I now consider loss for the sake of Christ. What is more, I consider everything a loss because of the surpassing worth of knowing Christ Jesus my Lord, for whose sake I have lost all things. I consider them garbage, *that I may gain Christ and be found in him.*" (Philippians 3:7-9, emphasis mine)

We lose our life so that we may gain Christ and be found in him. That's why Paul counts all his accomplishments as garbage. The Greek word for garbage in verse eight is *skubalon,* and it means "refuse," stuff that is not good for anything but the garbage heap or dung pile. The Message translates that word as "dog dung." There is no bigger life accomplishment than being found in Christ. Paul knew that, and it's why he said yes to God's divine invitation. No ifs, ands, or buts about it.

Journal Point: Is there an accomplishment in your life you feel defines you? Your marriage? Your home? You children? Your grandchildren? Your career? Your college degree? Write about how that makes you feel valuable.

Journal Point: Is there anything in your life that is holding you back from "losing your life" to follow God like Ruth gave up everything to follow Naomi? What is it?

Journal Point: What do you think Paul means when he says he is counting all his greatest accomplishments in life as garbage?

Digging Deeper:

For an increased understanding of the material in this chapter, I recommend you study the following passages using the SOAP method found in appendix 2 on page 145. Use your journal to record your studies.

- Matthew 16:24-27
- 2 Corinthians 4:7-18
- Philippians 1:15-20
- Philippians 3:7-14

Action Point:

1. One of the best ways to gain a deep appreciation of the life God has given you is to practice the habit of remembering what God has done. In your journal, start a list of things you know God has done in your life—places where you know he showed up. These may be small things or big things. Listen to the Holy Spirit about what to add to this list over time. Be sure and date each entry and make a point to commit some of the details to memory. These will become the stories of your legacy—places where God has intervened in your life, answered your prayers, brought a detour along that turned into a better road, or made you wait for His best. My list is simply called "Remember What God Has Done."

2. Read over this list from time to time. It will help you develop a heart of gratitude.

Chapter Four

YES, BUT—CLAUSES, CONDITIONS, AND CAVEATS

"But one thing I do: Forgetting what is behind and straining toward what is ahead, I press on toward the goal to win the prize for which God has called me heavenward in Christ Jesus."

PHILIPPIANS 3:13-14

"Therefore, there is now no condemnation for those who are in Christ Jesus, because through Christ Jesus the law of the Spirit who gives life has set you[a] free from the law of sin and death."

ROMANS 8:1-2

THE GOD WHO DOESN'T KEEP SCORE

When Peter asked Jesus how many times he had to forgive someone who offended him, Peter offered up a number he thought was pretty generous: "up to seven times" (Matthew 18:21). Jesus replied, "up to seventy times seven" (v. 22). He wasn't giving Peter a definitive number: 490. Instead, Jesus was inferring that God doesn't keep score. God perseveres.

This chapter is about the resiliency of a heavenly Father who calls us and then sticks with us when we hem and haw. It is about the perseverance of a God who won't let us go, who won't let us run away. It's about staying power when it gets uncomfortable; it's about grit in the face of fear. We're going to meet three people who answered the divine invitation after an objection or two… or more.

THE WOMAN AT THE WELL: A WALK OF SHAME

In the book of John, we meet a woman who had five husbands. And the man she was currently living with was not her husband. Today's culture may not blink twice at the life of the woman at the well in John 4. In Jesus' time, however, this woman hid in the shadows. She didn't want to be seen. She was shunned. Wives grabbed their husband's arm and hurried past, averting their eyes. Single women crossed the street to get away from her. Like the old country song by Johnny Lee, she was lookin' for love in all the wrong places.

But sister, God is not as interested in our past as we are. To him, our past does not determine our purpose. He can use our past for his purpose. All he wants is our heart. He'll do the rest.

Journal Point: Is there something in your past or some inadequacy you see in yourself that keeps you from thinking that God can use you for his glory? Describe what that is. We'll come back to this later in the chapter.

THE SET-UP: THE WRONG
PLACE AT THE RIGHT TIME

In the first few chapters of John, we see Jesus' ministry launching and gathering momentum in two very public events. First, he attended a wedding with his mother where he performed his first miracle. Then, while visiting the temple around Passover, he made a whip out of cords and drove out the merchandisers. The Jews publicly challenged his authority, and he made his first proclamation of his true identity (John 2:19). When word reached the Pharisees of his growing following, Jesus headed back to Galilee (4:3).

Jesus didn't bypass Samaria on his way to Galilee like many Jews would have done due to the division of the kingdoms since the days of Rehoboam (1 Kings 12). Instead, Jesus told his disciples he "had to go through Samaria on the way" (John 4:4). It turned out he had an appointment. When they got to Sychar, the disciples went into the town to buy food, and Jesus, weary from the journey, sat down at the community well outside the gates (v. 6). While he was there, a woman approached the well with an empty water jug. It was high noon—not the usual time women came to draw water.[1]

The Living Water Can Wash Away Our Shame

This woman arrived at midday for a reason. As she talked with Jesus, we see she had lived a life of bad choices—choices that probably carried a heavy load of shame. Sneaking to the well at the hottest part of the day helped her avoid the stares of the women who normally came at the cooler times of the day.

To get the conversation going, Jesus asked the woman for a drink of water. Her first objection was that she was a Samaritan, and Jews didn't talk to Samaritans. I have a feeling she added a caveat in her head thinking, "if he only knew the whole story."

Journal Point: Do you remember a time when someone asked you to serve or come to a gathering, but you backed away because you didn't want to risk people getting to know you better? How did you feel?

Jesus then began to soften her hard shell of shame with God's grace: "If you only knew the gift God has for you and who you are speaking to, you would ask me, and I would give you the living water" (John 4:10 NLT). Still not quite understanding what Jesus was saying, I think her mind jumped to a convenient conclusion: "Sir, give me this water so that I won't get thirsty and have to keep coming here to draw water" (v. 15). This stranger was giving her a way to never have to worry about her walk of shame to the well again.

Then Jesus asked her a question that lovingly put the focus on her shame without calling her out. He asked her to go and get her husband, knowing that she had already been married five times and was currently living with a man who was not her husband. Jesus didn't condemn her; he invited her to be redeemed. He gives us the same chance. He will touch that painful scar with a loving question, giving us a chance to bring our thirsty shame-filled souls to the Living Water.

> *Journal Point:* Remember that item from your past you identified at the beginning of the chapter? Is there anything that is stopping you from bringing that item from your past to Jesus to be washed away with his life-giving blood? Ask him right now to come into that memory and wash it clean. Ask him to set it apart and heal it with his living water.

THE DIVINE INVITATION

Jesus did not relent after he revealed her shame. He told her that the time had come when all people could worship the Father "in spirit and truth," breaking down the walls between Gentiles and Jews, women and men, righteous and fallen. The last remnant of shame was destroyed (vv. 23-24). Her heart began to open with the confession she knew the Messiah was coming to explain everything. Jesus walked through that opening with a personal invitation: "I, the one speaking to you—I am he" (v. 26).

This is one of the most powerful invitations of grace and mercy in the Bible. All of a sudden every piece of their conversation made sense. Jesus offered a permanent solution to her shame by breaking down every objection she threw at him. She had nowhere to go, nowhere to hide.

Journal Point: Are there things you want to accomplish before you give your life fully to God? Maybe you are not quite ready to surrender your whole agenda—your career, your children, your pocketbook, your friendships, your marriage—to God? Write a prayer in your journal asking God to reveal to you anything that is holding you back from fully engaging in his purpose for your life.

HER ANSWER: HER ASSIGNMENT

When Jesus' disciples returned, they were surprised to find him talking with a woman (v. 27). Their return was her cue to exit stage left. She left her water jug behind (v. 28), not because she was ashamed or startled but because she now had a purpose to fulfill. She had just encountered the Messiah face to face, and her life changed in an instant. She had been called and her answer was to go and tell. She went back to the town and said to the people, "Come and see a man who told me everything I ever did. Could this be the Messiah?" They came out of the town and made their way toward him (vs. 28-30).

There are two miraculous things to see here. First, she went back to town, back to the people who shunned her, who whispered about her behind her back, who had shamed her so maliciously that she avoided them all by sneaking out to get water at noon. I think she ran back, by the way. She was on a mission. Being freed from shame and guilt will embolden us. Embracing the truth about who we are will set us free (John 8:32).

Second, the people followed her out of town to find Jesus. They believed her. Have you ever been drawn to someone who is totally on fire for God? Does their passion inspire you? You can see it in their eyes. The people who used to shame her saw something in her that set a fire in their own souls.

God honored her change of heart with a purpose. "Many of the Samaritans from that town believed in him because of the woman's testimony" (v. 39). Jesus stayed with them for a two-day revival in which many more Samaritans became believers because they heard him speak, all because the woman at the well left her jug of past shame and fear to run and tell everyone she had found the Messiah. What a story of redemption. What amazing grace. Not only was she the first evangelist of record in the New Testament, but that special calling came to a woman whose sins were as bold as scarlet but had been washed away with Living Water. And that same Living Water is available for us today. There is nothing we have done that will separate us from that redeeming love. Read Romans 8:35-39 out loud. Jesus isn't interested in your past. Give him your heart and he will do the rest.

Journal Point: In what ways do you identify with the woman at well and her story?

ESTHER: FOR SUCH
A TIME AS THIS

"It looks like you're taking your ball and going home." I'll never forget those words my best friend spoke to me. The two years I had spent working towards my degree in pastoral leadership were almost over, and I was leaving town two days before the highly anticipated graduation ceremony. And all because somebody had hurt my feelings. She knew exactly what had happened and wanted me to own up to my actions. I was letting someone's mean words drive me away from something I'd been looking forward to for years. I was afraid to walk up on the stage knowing all my classmates and teachers had heard what was going on. I thanked my wise friend, put on my big girl pants, and toughed out the weekend.

Opposition goes with the territory when you're a child of the King. We have an enemy who wants to steal, kill, and destroy (John 10:10), and using people's fear is a common battle tactic. Esther was no stranger to fear. But she knew that opposition was just a detour not a dead end. She knew if God was in it, he would provide.

THE SET-UP:
AGAINST ALL ODDS

Esther was an orphan raised by her cousin Mordecai. He was a respected Jewish leader in a time when the Jews were in exile under Persian rule. The reigning queen of Persia had just been banished for refusing the king's command, and the hunt was on for a new queen. Mordecai put Esther forth as a candidate but made her swear not to reveal her ethnicity. He knew a Jewish woman would not find favor in the royal court. After twelve months of beauty treatments, Esther was chosen to be queen.

In the meantime, opposition was sowing seeds at the city gate. One of the king's officials, Haman, tricked the king into signing a decree that all Jews in the province should be executed because Mordecai refused to bow to him in public. When Mordecai found out, he sent a message to Esther to enlist her help.

THE DIVINE INVITATION: BUT GOD...

Mordecai filled Esther in on Haman's deception and asked Esther to petition the king for help. Esther reminded Mordecai that she may lose her life asking to come before the king uninvited, even though she was the queen. Esther didn't say no, but she clearly was afraid. Sometimes an invitation from God can carry a risk. But Mordecai, in his wisdom and experience, knew that Esther was made queen "for such a time as this" (Esther 4:14). He just needed to convince her.

When God's invitation plays into fear's hands, we need a wise voice to speak into our doubts. In times of trouble, surround yourself with voices of wisdom and truth.

Journal Point: Can you think of a time when someone's harsh words or selfish intentions stopped you from doing something you knew you should do? What happened?

Journal Point: Have you ever had a close friend talk you out of running away from something you were trying to avoid? How did that turn out?

ESTHER'S ANSWER: DO IT AFRAID

There is an old quote that says, "courage is not the absence of fear but rather the assessment that something else is more important than fear." And this was Esther's answer to Mordecai: "if I perish, I perish" (4:16). But Esther had a plan. She decided the way through was to turn the tables. She would deceive the deceiver. She hosted a couple banquets, buttered up the king, and when he asked her what she wanted, she pleaded for him to spare her life and the lives of her people (7:3-4). After the king learned of Haman's plan of death, he ordered him killed on the very pole Haman had built to kill Mordecai (7:10).

Don't ever be afraid of opposition. God did not give you a spirit of fear but one of power, love, and self-discipline (2 Timothy 1:7). If God is in it, he will provide (Ephesians 3:20).

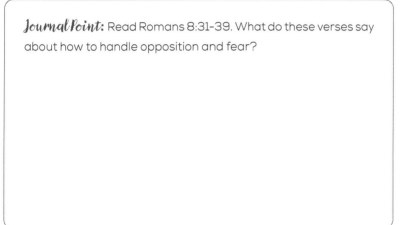

Journal Point: Read Romans 8:31-39. What do these verses say about how to handle opposition and fear?

THOUGHTS FOR OUR JOURNEY

I can relate to the woman at the well. Much of my adult life involved chasing accomplishments that I thought would shine brighter than my embarrassing past. Sometimes we think our past puts us in some kind of category of people who cannot be used by God. We start to chase things that make us feel good about *ourselves* instead of chasing a God who loves us just the way we are.

When we think we are unusable or need to hide who we really are, it's easy to think of the woman at the well and Esther as outliers instead of examples *we* can follow. Maybe you don't see yourself in their stories. But God hasn't called us to emulate their lives; he's called us to emulate their hearts. These women fulfilled impactful assignments for God, not because of who they were but because they said yes. Friend, if we are willing to say yes to God, he will give us assignment after assignment for his kingdom. All we need to do is bring a willing heart.

Digging Deeper:

For an increased understanding of the material in this chapter, I recommend you study the following passages using the SOAP method found in appendix 2 on page 145. Use your journal to record your studies.

- John 4:1-30
- Esther 4:11-16
- Isaiah 1: 18-20
- Luke 7:40-50

Action Points

1. One thing that can keep us from giving complete control of our disruptions and detours over to God is the fear that something bad will happen to us if we do. Oftentimes fear is rooted, not in unbelief but in lack of intimacy. We need to be closer to God in our everyday lives. We're going to start that journey to intimacy by making a list I call "O God, You Are…" It's a list of Scriptures I've found over the years that describes God's relationship with his children—that's us. We can lay claim to every single promise and truth on this list. Reciting this list daily from my heart has helped me to realize just how worthy God is of all my devotion and allegiance. Do it in a personal way. List each of these qualities in the first person and speak them as if the God of the universe is sitting right there with you… because he is.

2. I'll give you a starting point. Write these declarations and Scripture references in your journal and say them every day. Feel free to add to them anything you find helpful. When that journal fills up, take out those pages and put them in the new journal. I have come to rely on these daily confessions to remind me of just how wonderful God is and what he has given me. I know they will draw you closer to him as you recite them daily.

   - *O God, You are wise.* Your wisdom is pure, peace-loving, gentle at all times, and willing to yield to others. You have promised me your wisdom if I ask. (James 1:5, 3:17)

- *O God, You are holy.* Even when I am in trouble and when I feel abandoned, you are still holy. (Psalm 22:1-3)

- *O God, You are merciful.* How generous you are to offer me new mercies every morning. You are slow to anger and rich in love. (Lamentations 3:23, Psalm 145:8)

- *O God, You are just.* Your works are perfect, and all your ways are right. (Deuteronomy 32:4)

- *O God, You are my redeemer in trouble.* Whenever you test me, I will seek you. I will remember you are my rock and my most high redeemer. (Psalm 78:34-35)

- *O God, You are good.* I have tasted and seen that you are good. I am blessed when I take refuge in You. (Psalm 34:8)

- *O God, You are patient.* You are not slow in keeping your promise. Instead you are patient not wanting anyone to perish. (2 Peter 3:9)

- *O God, You are all knowing.* You have searched me and know me. You know when I sit and when I rise. Before a word is on my tongue you know it completely. You know what's best for me. (Psalm 139: 1-4)

- *O God, You are the giver of good things.* May I not put my hope in wealth, which is uncertain, but put my hope in you who richly provides me with everything for my enjoyment. (1 Timothy 6:17-18)

- *O God, your love in unfailing* and nothing in all creation will separate me from your love. (Romans 8:39)

Chapter Five

WHY ME?

*"Continue to work out your salvation with fear and trembling, for it is good
who works in you to will and to act in order to fulfill his good purpose."*

PHILIPPIANS 2:12-13

*"Being confident of this, that he who began a good work in you
will carry it on to completion until the day of Christ Jesus."*

PHILIPPIANS 1:6

DON'T DESPISE SMALL BEGINNINGS

I found Peter, scrawny and scared, eyes still not open, crying under a tree. This skinny newborn kitten had been separated from his mother somehow and ended up in my yard under my tree. I was just leaving for work when I heard his distress call. My heart melted, so I grabbed an old cat carrier and dropped him at the vet on my way into town. I remember telling them if they could keep him alive, I'd be back to pick him up after work. When I returned after work, they had revived him, given him a couple shots, and sent me home with an eye dropper, a supply of powdered milk, and a sheet of instructions. That little fella became my constant companion for twelve years. In his life he tangled with a mountain lion, numerous pheasants, neighboring cats and dogs, and a racoon. We took many trips to the vet. He was a fearless fifteen-pound ginger tabby that didn't have an ounce of fat on his powerful body. He and I went through a lot together over the years. His meager beginnings became my magnificent blessing.

MOSES: A BAG FULL OF EXCUSES

When you survey the life of Moses in the Old Testament, it's hard to believe that his meager beginning in the first three chapters of Exodus is the same

Moses in chapter 14. But before we get ahead of ourselves, a little background is necessary.

Moses was born during a time when the Israelites were enslaved by the Egyptians. The Hebrews had grown great in number. Pharaoh feared they might revolt, so he ordered all male babies drowned. Moses' sister hid him in a basket by the river where he would be discovered and raised by one of Pharaoh's daughters. Moses was aware of his humble beginnings (Exodus 2:11), and one day he came upon a Hebrew being beaten by an Egyptian taskmaster. After checking to make sure no one was looking, he killed the Egyptian and buried him in the sand. When Pharaoh found out, he tried to kill Moses, but Moses fled to Midian. Now this wasn't an overnight journey; it was about two hundred miles just to the border of Midian as the crow flies. We don't know exactly where in Midian he was or why he went there, but it was a long way from Egypt. It was a place to disappear and start a new life.

THE SET-UP

At Midian Moses helped some maidens water their father's flock. This led to an invitation to supper, which turned into a life of obscurity as a shepherd for the next forty years (Exodus 2:20-21). Moses even named his firstborn son Gershom, which meant "I have become a foreigner in a foreign land" (Exodus 2:22). Moses led a quiet life tending sheep for his father-in-law. One day he led the sheep to the far side of the wilderness by Mount Horeb, the location where he would return some years later to receive the Ten Commandments.[2] It was there that his lack of confidence and feelings of failure came face-to-face with the living God.

Journal Point: What events in Exodus 1-2 could have contributed to Moses' willingness to settle for an obscure life in Midian? Is there something on that list you can identify with?

THE LONG-SUFFERING DIVINE INVITATION

In Exodus 3, we see the beginning of Moses' interaction with the burning bush. We see in verses two and three that Moses was curious about why the bush didn't burn up, so he walked over to see what was going on. In verse two *we* are told that the angel of the Lord is in the bush, but Moses doesn't seem to recognize that… yet. It had been a long time since Moses was part of a culture that worshipped Yahweh. It is no wonder that he initially thought of the burning bush only as some kind of curiosity.

> **Journal Point:** Is it easy for us to believe that the everyday occurrences in our life are just stuff that happens? How can we be more alert to God's presence?

When God called to Moses and identified himself (vs. 4-6), he told Moses to keep his distance and take off his sandals. After realizing that Yaweh was calling him, Moses immediately hid his face from God. It is a dangerous thing to be in the presence of something so holy. Moses didn't know what to expect. God didn't waste any time getting to the point:

> The LORD said, "I have indeed seen the misery of my people in Egypt. I have heard them crying out because of their slave drivers, and I am concerned about their suffering. So I have come down to rescue them from the hand of the Egyptians and to bring them up out of that land into a good and spacious land, a land flowing with milk and honey—the home of the Canaanites, Hittites, Amorites, Perizzites, Hivites and Jebusites. And now the cry of the Israelites has reached me, and I have seen the way the Egyptians are oppressing

them. So now, go. I am sending you to Pharaoh to bring my people the Israelites out of Egypt." (Exodus 3:7-10)

Let's stop here for a moment and get inside Moses' head. He had been living in anonymity for most of his adult life. He finally had a nice little life. He must have been wondering if God had him confused with someone else. After all, isn't he the one who killed he Egyptian official and ran off? Is this a punishment? Is God sending him to be killed after all these years? This must be some kind of a mistake, right?

THE ANSWER(S): RUNNING OUT OF EXCUSES

In the television series *The Office* there is a character named Ryan Howard who has an aspiration to move from sales to management in the famous Dunder Mifflin paper company. In season three, Ryan reveals his skill at finding an excuse for everything when he is asked to go to lunch with the boss. He quickly lists several excuses in a run-on sentence of why he can't go including work to do, MSG and peanut allergies, and "I just ate there last night." As his co-worker Jim Halpert sarcastically thanks him for using all the excuses, Howard spiels off several more he could have used and picks us his cell phone saying, "use your head, man. I keep mine in here."

Making excuses can be an art form, and Moses seemed to be an artiste. Excuse number one: *"But why me? What makes you think that I could ever go to Pharaoh and lead the children of Israel out of Egypt?"* (Exodus 3:11 MSG).

Given Moses' background, I think this is a logical question. It sounds like something I would say. How about you? Now God's answer in verse 12 set a pattern for the rest of the exchange. Moses' objections were about him and his lack of abilities; God's answers were about what he could do. This was key because we do the same thing. When God puts something in front of us to do, our first reaction is, "but I can't do that." But God said to Moses:

> "I'll be with you," God said. "And this will be the proof that I am the one who sent you: When you have brought my people out of Egypt, you will worship God right here at this very mountain." (3:12)

Excuse number two: *What happens if the Israelites don't believe me or want to follow me out of Egypt?* Surely some of Moses' contemporaries were still alive and would remember who he was and what he had done. He had no street cred.

As a matter of fact, he was a runaway convict, and he wanted to know how to answer the question *Who sent you?*

Journal Point: Can you think of a time in the past when an opportunity came up and you used an excuse (your age, lack of skill or education, you don't feel prepared, or fear of doing a new thing) to get out of it? Explain what stopped you from going forward.

Using the same pattern, God's answer took Moses' eyes off who he was and what he could do and focused on *who* God is and what *he* can do."

> "I am who I am. This is what you are to say to the Israelites: 'I am has sent me to you…. Say to the Israelites, 'The Lord, the God of your fathers—the God of Abraham, the God of Isaac and the God of Jacob—has sent me to you.' This is my name forever, the name you shall call me from generation to generation." (Exodus 3:14-15)

In verses 16-22 God gave Moses some specific promises to give to the elders of Israel, so they would buy in too. And he also told Moses to take the elders with him when he went to see Pharaoh. Moses needed some flesh-and-blood help to give him confidence, right?

Excuse number three: *What if they don't believe me?* God could see Moses' confidence melting with each passing moment, so he gave him a series of miracles he could perform to prove he was being sent from God. In Exodus 4:2-8 God ran Moses through a dress rehearsal of all the supernatural events that would prove he was legit. And if that didn't work, the final feat would involve turning river water into blood.

Moses has one more objection. Excuse number four: *Pardon your servant, Lord. I have never been eloquent, neither in the past nor since you have spoken to your servant. I am slow of speech and tongue.* Are you starting to see the pattern? First Moses wanted to know the plan. When he found out, it terrified him and he threw out what he thought were deal-breakers. But God wasn't having any of it. He said it as plain as he could:

> Who gave human beings their mouths? Who makes them deaf or mute? Who gives them sight or makes them blind? Is it not I, the LORD? Now go; I will help you speak and will teach you what to say. (Exodus 4:11-12)

Moses realized he had no more excuses, so he just came out with it—in a polite way: "Pardon your servant, Lord. Please send someone else" (v. 13). Moses wanted out of the deal.

God knew this was coming. His anger burned against Moses and he said:

> What about your brother, Aaron the Levite? I know he can speak well. He is already on his way to meet you, and he will be glad to see you. You shall speak to him and put words in his mouth; I will help both of you speak and will teach you what to do. He will speak to the people for you, and it will be as if he were your mouth and as if you were God to him. But take this staff in your hand so you can perform the signs with it. (Exodus 4:14-17)

Not What I Hoped it Would Be

I don't know about you, but this is a sad ending to the conversation for me. I so wanted Moses to rise up and go in courage. I was cheering for him, but it didn't happen. How often do we bypass the fullness of God's wonderful plan for us because we can't get over the hump of self-confidence? In my own life, more often than I'd like to admit.

Life often throws something at us that we just don't want to face. Disruptions and detours are unwanted. Let's just get that out there. But the truth of the matter is, disruptions are the path to purpose. They are growth agents, opportunities to grow more like God and closer to God. Moses finally said yes to God but not until he rambled through a litany of excuses and finally told God he preferred to stay at home with his nice little life. We can gauge his lack of excitement when we read how he returned to his father-in-law and said, "Let me return to my own people in Egypt to see if any of them are still alive" (v. 18). Not exactly the truth, but it was a good excuse to go.

Journal Point: How do you feel about disruptions? Read James 1:2-4. What do you think James is saying here when he tells us to "consider it pure joy whenever you face trials of many kinds"? Do you think it's possible to have joy in the middle of trials?

THOUGHTS FOR OUR JOURNEY

Remember when I said in the beginning of this chapter that it's hard to believe that Moses' meager beginning in the first three chapters of Exodus is the same Moses in chapter 14? Before we leave Moses in a puddle of discouragement, let's take a look at what happened after God used Moses and Aaron to finally free the Jews from Pharaoh's grip. In Exodus 14 we read about how the Egyptian officials realized they made a mistake by letting Israel go. So they mounted up a huge army and took off to bring the Jews back. When the Israelites saw them coming, doubt came rushing in, and they began to challenge Moses' mission from God:

> Was it because there were no graves in Egypt that you brought us to the desert to die? What have you done to us by bringing us out of Egypt? Didn't we say to you in Egypt, 'Leave us alone; let us serve the Egyptians'? It would have been better for us to serve the Egyptians than to die in the desert! (Exodus 14:11-12)

The old Moses would have started wringing his hands, stuttering, and looking nervously at Aaron for something to say. Up until that point, everything

Moses said to the people had been only what God told him to say. But for the first time since God called him, Moses stood up and became the eloquent encourager God called him to be:

> Moses answered the people, "Do not be afraid. Stand firm and you will see the deliverance the LORD will bring you today. The Egyptians you see today you will never see again. The LORD will fight for you; you need only to be still." (Exodus 14:13-14)

And the rest is history.

Friend, the same God who transformed Moses from his meager beginning into a magnificent blessing can do the same for you. No matter what disruption you're facing, what you think you can and can't do, our God is able. God is a God of small beginnings: "Do not despise these small beginnings, for the LORD rejoices to see the work begin" (Zechariah 4:10 NLT).

He will take whatever you're up against, whatever excuses you have, and use it as the impetus to keep you running the race he has marked out for you. "So take a new grip with your tired hands and strengthen your weak knees. Mark out a straight path for your feet so that those who are weak and lame will not fall but become strong" (Hebrews 12:12-13 NLT).

> Therefore, since we are surrounded by such a huge crowd of witnesses to the life of faith, let us strip off every weight that slows us down, especially the sin that so easily trips us up. And let us run with endurance the race God has set before us. We do this by keeping our eyes on Jesus, the champion who initiates and perfects our faith. Because of the joy awaiting him, he endured the cross, disregarding its shame. Now he is seated in the place of honor beside God's throne. Think of all the hostility he endured from sinful people; then you won't become weary and give up. (Hebrews 12:1-3 NLT)

Digging Deeper:

For an increased understanding of the material in this chapter, I recommend you study the following passages using the SOAP method found in appendix 2 on page 145. Use your journal to record your studies.

- Philippians 1:3-8
- Hebrews 12:1-3
- Joshua 1:5-10
- Ephesians 3:16-21

Action Points:

1. Is there something you feel God has been nudging you to do but for whatever reason you've been putting him off? Is there a detour in the way? Is it disrupting your life? Is there something you need to give up? Something you really want to do but can't seem to find the time? It could be something like joining the church prayer team. Or maybe volunteering one day a week at the local food bank. Maybe you have a book in you or a song? Maybe your TV watching habits are sending you to bed with violence or perversion on your heart? Maybe God has been giving you a burden for a neighbor that you really don't know very well? It may be more than one thing. Whatever it is start writing about it in your journal. How much time would it take? What does it involve doing that frightens you? What's in your bag of excuses? Write them down too.

2. The next step is prayer. Take this narrative to God. Put it on your prayer list for the next thirty days. Enlist a trusted friend to pray with you. Do you need the Chain Breaker or the Waymaker to come alongside you?

3. Next, if all the impediments to accomplishing this act of service for God were removed, what would your life look like? What is the first step you need to take to make this a reality. Don't let what you're afraid of keep you from what you were made for. Write down your thoughts.

4. And lastly, borrowing some advice from one of my favorite authors, Bob Goff: "Don't worry about all the steps. Begin. No one is remembered for what they just plan to do."[3]

Chapter Six

REFRAMING AND REBUILDING-WHERE WE GO FROM HERE

"These words I speak to you are not incidental additions to your life, homeowner improvements to your standard of living. They are foundational words, words to build a life on. If you work these words into your life, you are like a smart carpenter who built his house on solid rock. Rain poured down, the river flooded, a tornado hit—but nothing moved that house. It was fixed to the rock. But if you just use my words in Bible studies and don't work them into your life, you are like a stupid carpenter who built his house on the sandy beach. When a storm rolled in and the waves came up, it collapsed like a house of cards."

MATTHEW 7:24-27 MSG

"So here's what I want you to do, God helping you: Take your everyday, ordinary life—your sleeping, eating, going-to-work, and walking-around life—and place it before God as an offering. Embracing what God has done for you is the best thing you can do for him. Don't become so well-adjusted to your culture that you fit into it without even thinking. Instead, fix your attention on God. You'll be changed from the inside out. Readily recognize what he wants from you, and quickly respond to it. Unlike the culture around, always dragging you down to its level of immaturity, God brings the best out of you, develops well-formed maturity in you."

ROMANS 12:1-2 MSG

In 1979, the Public Broadcasting Service (PBS) launched a television show that ignited our love affair with home improvement shows. *This Old House*, based in the Boston area, specialized in renovating old houses. Forty-one seasons later and still going, *This Old House* is the original seed of over fifty shows and multiple networks in the home improvement genre. We clearly have a love affair with reframing and rebuilding.

Just like an old house, when we set out to update and reframe beliefs that we've lived in for years, we need to start with a plan. Reframing our idea of the abundant life will also take some elbow grease. Old walls don't come down easily. It could be your house just needs some paint, some refreshing to get a new perspective. But it could be you need to tear some walls down and start all over again. Wherever you are in life, God's got you covered. And he is going to change you from the inside out (Proverbs 3:5-6). And just like on *This Old House*, we'll start by looking at the foundation.

HOW FIRM IS YOUR FOUNDATION?

In Matthew 7:24-27 Jesus lays out the truth about how we should build our lives. And his words are not suggestions. They are not "home improvements" to our nice little lives. They are bedrock, the best material on which we can build a foundation. A house built on bedrock will never fall down no matter what life throws at it. But he warns us that if we treat his words like divine suggestions, we are building our lives on sand—lives that will collapse like a house of cards when a storm rolls in. I love The Message interpretation: "But if you just use my words in Bible studies and don't work them into your life, you are like a stupid carpenter who built his house on the sandy beach" (Matthew 7:26-27).

There is no way to sugarcoat this truth. Jesus' words are not just words we study. They are words we need to live by. If we think our culture's idea of abundant life—chasing a life of ease—is better than chasing God's truth, then we are building on sinking sand.

So our first order of business is to look, I mean really look, at our idea of the role of trouble in our lives. Do we really believe Romans 8:28 is true for us at all times? Just in case you need a refresher, read this out loud: "And I know that all things work together for my good; for those who are called according to His purpose."

Is that true for all times, for all people? Yes, my friend. You are not the exception. No matter what you've gone through in life, it is true. Where we get into trouble with this verse, and what the enemy wants us to believe, is that it says all things *are* good. Nothing is further from the truth. All things are not good. The Bible does not teach that. Trouble is not easy. Trials are not a Disney ride. Disruption is not a Sunday drive. Life is not one smiling thirty-second commercial after another. Life is full of disruptions, detours, trials, and disappointments. Anyone who tells us different is lying. All things *work together* for our good. That, my friend, is the truth.

Two things play into this truth. First, the world is an evil place under the dominion of a powerful enemy. It's not our home; we're just passing through. Second, we make bad choices on occasion. We still have a sinful nature to contend with. But what the enemy intended to harm us with, God intends for our good (Genesis 50:20). God can use anything and everything to bring us closer to him. We just have to believe that is his intention. If God is for us, who can be against us? (Romans 8:31).

Journal Point: Read Romans 8:28 from several different Bible versions. You can do this at biblegateway.com or use the YouVersion app, if you have it. What is your biggest hurdle to believing this verse is true for you? Is there something you've gone through in life that is an exception to this truth? What happened?

Journal Point: What about things that happen in life that are so horrendous we can't seem to find healing? Instead of throwing away what you don't understand or like, can you trust God in that gap of your understanding? (Isaiah 55:8). Pray for God to show you the first steps to reconciling this situation to his love for you.

THE LONG GAME

So what do we do in light of our new foundation when we read what James wrote: "Consider it pure joy my brothers whenever you face trials of many kinds" (James 1:2)? I like what the New Living Translation says here: "consider it a great opportunity."

James wasn't writing this because he thought trials and trouble should be fun. He knew the deep consequences of perseverance. The onset of trouble ushers in the long game of becoming mature and complete, not lacking anything (James 1:4). I like the saying "troubles are a trigger." I also love the fact that James follows up this section in chapter one with a promise: if we need wisdom about this trouble, all we have to do is ask God, and he will give us that wisdom "generously to all without finding fault" (v. 5). God has every single base of our trouble covered.

NO-HOLDS-BARRED

The phrase *no-holds-barred* is another way of saying there are no rules. It originated in the sport of wrestling in the mid-twentieth century when amateur wrestling matches drew large crowds. Legal wrestling holds were regulated by rules that were suspended at these fan-favorite matches held in carnival atmospheres.

When we fully embrace our everyday, ordinary lives, we are living no-holds-barred lives. Small disruptions—the hurtful social media comment, the broken garbage disposal, and the party invite we didn't get are our proving ground. When we give our life to Jesus, we are agreeing to a no-holds-barred life. Every disruption, no matter what the size, is an invitation to lie down in green pastures, to be led beside still waters in the dark valley (Psalm 23:1-3). In that dark valley God restores our soul and works maturity and completeness into our lives. When the desire to be complete in Christ takes over the desire to duck when trouble comes, that is when God puts our faith life on fast-forward.

Two are Better Than One: Find Your Elizabeths

After Mary told God, "I am the Lord's servant. May your word to me be fulfilled" (Luke 1:38), do you remember what she did next? She didn't run home to her family or go see her beloved-to-be Joseph. She hurried off to see her cousin Elizabeth. When you decide to live a life where you embrace disruption, the way can feel hard and lonely. It's not your average go-to-church-every-Sunday kind of life. It requires a listening spirit and a heart open to whatever God brings your way. That kind of life needs like-minded company.

In Ecclesiastes 4:9-12 we see the definition of true spiritual friendship:

> Two are better than one, because they have a good return for their labor: If either of them falls down, one can help the other up. But pity anyone who falls and has no one to help them up. Also, if two lie down together, they will keep warm. But how can one keep warm alone? Though one may be overpowered, two can defend themselves. But how can one keep warm alone? Though one may be overpowered, two can defend themselves.

There are fifty-nine "one another" Scriptures in the New Testament. It's clear that the spiritual life is best lived in communion with others. The phrase is derived from the Greek word *allelon,* which means "each other," "mutual," and "reciprocal." In the Bible study *Women Finishing Well,* I called these sister-in-Christ friends, or SIC friends for short; they are women who have a mutual goal of encouraging each other to become more like Jesus. They listen to your dreams, comfort you in your hurts, call you on the carpet if need be, and ask the right questions without giving you all the answers. They are the women you run to when all hell breaks loose. The women you lean on in times of grief and sorrow. The women you do life with. Everyone needs an Elizabeth in their life. Surviving a life of disruption and detour will be almost impossible without like-minded girlfriends. Get you some if you haven't got them already. Determine to spend time together and keep connected, even if it's online or by phone. These are times when we are tempted to pull back and deal with our everyday overload alone. Don't do it. Keep connected, keep pursuing. You need one another.

Don't Ever Give Up

The truth is, living the abundant life can be scary. Esther was so scared when Mordecai asked her to go before the king and save the Jews that she reminded him she could lose her life. But she did it anyway. Moses had a bag of excuses, but he went back to Egypt anyway and was used by God to bring Israel to the shore of the promised land. The woman at the well had been married five times, and yet she became the first evangelist in the New Testament. Hannah had been barren and bullied until she almost lost hope of ever having a child. And then there was Samuel.

The Bible is filled with stories of real people like you and me who received an invitation from God to answer the call of a disrupted life. Start by embracing your everyday, ordinary life—your eating, sleeping, going-to-work, walking-around, and staying-at-home life. It will be full of disruptions, but it's the best thing you can do for God (Rom. 12:1 MSG).

Digging Deeper:

For an increased understanding of the material in this chapter, I recommend you study the following passages using the SOAP method found in appendix 2 on page 145. Use your journal to record your studies.

- Matthew 7:24-27 (from The Message version)
- Romans 12:9-21
- James 1:2-8 (from The Message version)
- John 15:9-17

Action Point:

1. Keep going. You've got more to do! Read on.

WHAT'S NEXT?
DON'T STOP NOW

So many times we read wonderful books and powerful Bible studies only to put them on the shelf and move on to the next one. It is my hope that you will stick with me for another thirty days while we explore together how to embrace the disruptions and detours God puts in our lives. There is an abundance of books on how to change a habit in thirty days. It might work for some things but not for making a major spiritual shift in your living. These thirty days of devotions are just the beginning. They are designed to keep you immersed in the process of that major spiritual shift. Embracing disruption is a lifelong mindset.

My journey to the abundant life began right after I got married—forty-two years ago—and I'm still working on it! Before you lose heart, let me confess that I spent the first thirty of those years running away from God's calling. Oh, I knew I was called, but I wanted to call the shots. When the going got tough, I wanted to run away—and even tried it a couple times, literally. So when it comes to going around the mountain, I've been around more times than I can count.

The abundant life is a journey that starts with a commitment. For the next thirty days, I ask you to spend some time with me studying, praying, listening, contemplating, and worshipping around this theme of embracing disruptions and getting into the mindset that disruptions are a good thing. I recommend you continue using your study journal for this daily reflection. Each devotion should take you about fifteen minutes. As a former high school teacher, I can tell you that consistent reviewing will make a huge difference in how readily you put this idea of abundant life into practice. "Do not merely listen to the word, and so deceive yourselves. Do what it says" (James 1:22).

In *Women Finishing Well* I introduced the Five Ws, a guide for connecting with God each morning. In these thirty days of devotions, we are going to use three of those Ws:

- **Word** is a time of study and personal interaction with a specific Bible passage. If you'd like to dig deeper, I recommend using the SOAP method of study we used in the Digging Deeper sections of the book.

- **Wait** is a time of personal connection with God in prayer.

- **Worship** is reflecting on the day's reading with music or song lyrics. I recommend searching online for videos of the recommended songs.

Over the next thirty days, you'll laugh, you'll cry, and you'll be challenged. Don't be tempted to take more than one day at a time. Stay at each day's mile marker. Meditate on each day's devotion; let it all sink in. Let God speak into your heart about your own personal journey to abundant life. But most of all, God has promised he will continue to work in you if you listen and come with a willing heart (Philippians 2:13). How about we continue this journey together? Let's lock arms and get started.

Note: Worship songs include a link to a YouTube lyric video when available. Some of these videos have ads at the beginning that you can skip after a few seconds. Be sure and look up each song and worship along!

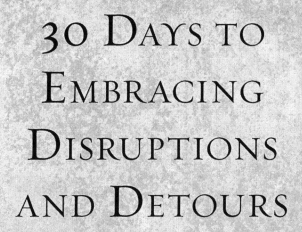

30 Days to Embracing Disruptions and Detours

Day 1

CRUISE CONTROL

Word: Read Luke 1:26-37 and Psalm 46:10.

My first taste of stop-and-go driving came the first winter my husband and I spent in San Diego. Driving in the wide-open spaces of Montana's two-lane roads where we farm, I was addicted to my cruise control. I used to joke that I could read a book while driving on the interstate in eastern Montana. It was in stark contrast to the hectic pace of on the southern California freeways. Paying attention to the abruptly changing speeds on the I-5 consumed all my attention.

Mary's life was turned upside down by an angel's declaration that she would give birth to a son... as a virgin. She went from cruise control to a dead stop in one moment. And she was troubled (v. 29). It's okay to be momentarily thrown for a loop by a disruption. We are human. It's not a sign we are bad people or have no faith; it's a sign that God is working in us. It's a sign that he wants to take the wheel. It's a sign he wants us to listen, and it may involve a tussle.

Disruptions are a part of our Christian growth. There is no going forward into what God wants us to be without going backward occasionally. There are things in us God wants to refine, and some things he wants to remove. What we *won't* see in the disruption is God's final purpose. We know that all things work together for our good, but we don't know how. And sometimes that drives us crazy. Sometimes we just want to put the pedal to the metal and go, and God says, "Be still and know that I am God" (Psalm 46:10).

When we turn our hearts to listening and remember that God is for us, we can confidently say, "I am the Lord's servant. May everything you have said about me come true."

Wait in prayer: What is sticking out to you in today's Bible reading? How is your life on cruise control? Write out a prayer asking God to help you be fearless in the face of disruption. Remind yourself that nothing formed against you will stand (Isaiah 54:17).

Worship: Listen to "Whom Shall I Fear" performed by Chris Tomlin.

Day 2

DID GOD REALLY SAY?

Word: Read Genesis 3:1-7.

Same old, same old. When Eve encountered the serpent in the garden, the question the snake posed was a question he is still hissing today: "did God really say…?" The enemy twists the Word of God into a lie in order to steal, kill, and destroy. His arsenal includes a number of weapons but the most effective by far is the half-truth. We see him use this weapon skillfully in Genesis 3:4-5. The half-truth on the front of his statement is punched with the lie on the back. And that lie is his gem because it speaks to a deep desire in our proud souls: you can be like God.

Three things attracted Eve to the apple. Two of them seemed harmless: it looked good to eat and was pleasing to the eye. The garden was loaded with food that checked those two boxes. The third thing that drew her to the apple spoke to her pride: "she wanted the wisdom it would give her" (Genesis 3:6).

Isn't that just like us today? We want the wisdom to run our own life, to make our own decisions, to grab hold of the wheel. Wouldn't that be magical, to have the knowledge to create a perfect life? That's what drew Eve to take that bite.

As we go through these thirty days, you'll be challenged to give up some half-truths the enemy has been feeding you about disruption and detours. He wants to convince you to keep both hands on the wheel of your life. May God give you wisdom for the journey and courage to let go of your half-truths and embrace the whole truth and nothing but the truth.

Wait in prayer: Write out a prayer asking Jesus to reveal places in your life where you are accepting half-truths and identify them by name. Pray that you would know the whole truth and nothing but the truth about this area of your life. Pray that you will know the truth and that it would set you free (John 8:32).

Worship: Listen to "Voice of Truth" performed by Casting Crowns.

Day 3

A NICE LITTLE LIFE

Word: Read John 10:10 and 2 Corinthians 4:16-18.

When I was a high school English teacher, one of my biggest frustrations was gifted students who did just enough to get by. No matter how interesting or engaging I made the class, they just settled for a C instead of the A they were capable of. They weren't lazy, just satisfied with not engaging with the learning process. I always chalked it up to typical teenage apathy some kids have for school.

Sometimes I wonder if we have become apathetic about our spiritual growth. In today's Scripture, we sit in on a discussion Jesus had with the Pharisees about the difference between Satan's mission and his. "The thief comes only to steal, kill, and destroy," Jesus told the religious leaders. And the path to that destruction is nothing violent or traumatic. The prime tactic the enemy uses to destroy us is to get us to settle for a nice little life. The inherent danger is that a nice little life encourages us to forget there is something more, something Jesus promised in the second half of verse 10: abundant life to the full. The New Living Translation calls it "a rich and satisfying life." This life isn't defined by externals: a nice house, a couple cars, good kids, good health, and a vacation every year. It is an internal abiding relationship with a God who walks with us 24/7. It may include some of those externals, but it is never defined by them.

Paul put this in perspective for us in his second letter to the Corinthians when he told them not to lose heart because our light and momentary disruptions are working for us an eternal glory that far outweighs any nice little life the world can give us (2 Corinthians 4:16-18). So what do we need to do? We fix our eyes not on what is seen because what is seen (the nice little life) is temporary, but *what is not seen,* is eternal. That which is not seen, my friend, is the abundant life Jesus wants to give us. It is exceedingly, abundantly above and beyond anything we can dare ask or think (Ephesians 3:20).

Wait in prayer: Are you in danger of settling for a nice little life, a life of ease? Write a prayer asking Jesus to help you seek the life he has to offer—life to the full. Ask him to show you areas where you are starting to accept the status quo and not push through to the best life you can live in him. Ask him to give you a new attitude toward your "light and momentary troubles." Nothing we go through in this world can compare to the glory that is being revealed in us (Romans 8:18).

Worship: Listen to "Fix My Eyes" performed by For King and Country.

Day 4

WIN THE
SPIRITUAL LOTTERY

Word: Read Ephesians 1:3-14.

Have you ever bought a lottery ticket? I'm ashamed to admit I have—several of them. I went through a period in my life where we were having financial trouble—lean years on the farm—and I was getting weary. I had it all worked out with God. If he would give me a winning lottery ticket, I would use it to pay off all our debt, my family's debt, put some in our savings account, and give the rest away. Sounds like a holy deal, right? All good?

One day I was studying Ephesians 1:3-14 and verse three would not leave me alone: "Praise be to the God and Father of our Lord Jesus Christ, who has blessed me in the heavenly realms with every spiritual blessing in Christ." Not some blessings but *every* blessing. So what are the blessings we have in Christ, anyway? I made a list:

- We were chosen in Jesus before the creation of the world. (v. 4)

- We are holy and blameless in his sight. (v. 4)

- We have been predestined (in love) to be adopted as his children to show the world his glory. (vv. 5-6)

- We are redeemed and forgiven by grace we do not deserve—it's been lavished on us. (vv. 7-8)

- He's made known the mystery of his will to us. (v. 9)

- We have a predestined place in his plan. (v. 11)

- I have been given the Holy Spirit as a seal of my redemption—God lives in me. (vv. 13-14)

I had to camp there for a few days before I realized just how rich these blessings are. Those verses made such an impact on my life that I wrote them out in the first person and say them every day. We can never lose sight of who we are in Jesus. He died so I could receive those blessings. Think of them, meditate on them, remind yourself of them every single day. I encourage you to start each day with this list. And open with verse three: "Praise be to the God and Father of my Lord Jesus Christ, who has blessed me in the heavenly realms with every spiritual blessing in Christ." We've won the spiritual lottery, my friend. Let's celebrate!

Wait in prayer: Thank God today for every spiritual blessing in Christ. As you read through verses 3-14 personalize each blessing. Ask God to work in you a humble attitude of gratitude for each one.

Worship: Listen to "How Great Is Our God" performed by Chris Tomlin.

Day 5

WRENCH IN THE WORKS

Word: Read James 1:2-8.

When my children were little, they both managed to catch strep throat. It seems like once it starts making the rounds at school, everybody gets a turn. The doctor prescribed a liquid antibiotic and its taste, even laced with fruity sugar, left something to be desired. I remember negotiating each dose by reminding them not that it was good for them but it was the path to getting back to their school friends. Sometimes extolling the benefits of what is good for us isn't enough to change anything.

We have that same feeling when God throws a wrench in our works with an unexpected disruption. Lots of times our first reaction is to ask, "why this, why now?" We might search for something we did wrong or something that was done to us. But God's purpose in disruption is not punishment, even though it tastes bad in out spirit. His purpose is to force our faith "into the open" (James 1:3 MSG). James even goes as far saying tests and trials are an "opportunity for great joy" (James 1:2, NLT). This is tough to do unless we are grounded in the truth of verses three and four: "because you know that the testing of your faith develops perseverance. Let perseverance finish its work *so that* you may be mature and complete, not lacking anything." I struggled with the "so that" for many years because I took my eyes off God's goal and focused on my own discomfort. Sometimes those two words still touch a nerve, depending on the test. But God's goal with every wrench thrown into my works is the same yesterday, today, and tomorrow: that I may be mature and complete, not lacking anything. Wow! *Not lacking anything.* That is the abundant life. But guess how we get there? Letting perseverance finish its work by being in step with God's Spirit (Galatians 5:25).

Wait in prayer: What is your biggest challenge to persevering through trouble? Write out a prayer today asking God to help you with that challenge. Commit yourself to listening and stepping out in faith regarding that challenge.

Worship: Listen to "Trust in You" performed by Lauren Daigle.

Day 6

CLEARING
THE FOOTPATH

Word: Read Hebrews 12:7-13 (from The Message version).

When I was growing up, summer vacations always meant piling in the car and making the long trek north to my grandparent's cabin in northern Wisconsin on Big Lake. On the prairie, lakes are few and far between, so when my kids got old enough to travel without car seats, I talked my husband into buying a small cabin on a wooded lake right across the Canadian border from our farm.

The cabin was set back from the water's edge, so our first order of business was clearing a footpath down to the water. Evidently the previous owners never went near the water. Grass that hasn't been mowed or walked on for years has several layers to deal with. First you have to cut the grass short enough to dethatch it with a bush mower. Those wispy waves of prairie grass were hiding a couple layers of compressed grass that needed clearing. The first layer was the hard stalks of grass that had years to gain strength. They felt like little swords poking into your legs. Under that was a dense layer of decomposing grass that had been crowded out by the stronger stalks over the years. And last but not least was the uneven ground that was peppered with gopher holes. This needed to be smoothed, sprayed to inhibit weed growth, and covered with a layer of small pea gravel. Clearing a footpath was hard work.

The writer of Hebrews reminds us that hard work, or discipline, is never fun or easy (Hebrews 12:4-11). *Discipline*, like the word *disruption*, can be cause for pause. Do we really want to do all this hard work God asked us to do? The answer, of course, is yes. Like the benefits we find in James 1:2-4, Hebrews 12 promises us that our hard work of clearing the path will "pay off handsomely"

(v. 11 MSG). The writer tells us not to "sit around on your hands! No more dragging your feet. Clear the path for the long-distance runners so no one will trip and fall, so no one will step in a hole and sprain an ankle. Help each other out. And run for it" (vv. 12-13 MSG).

Learning to embrace disruption and detours is not just for *our* own good. It is for all those who are running the path with us. Our family, friends, neighbors, and whoever is doing life with us. As we clear the footpath, we are making a smooth way for others. "For the entire law is fulfilled in keeping this one command: 'Love your neighbor as yourself' " (Galatians 5:14). God has given us people to run with. Help each other out. And run for it!

Wait in prayer: Is there a layer of underbrush you need to clear out so you can run your race without hindrances? Write out a prayer today asking God to help you clear the footpath for others. Write it in the first person like you're talking with God face-to-face and not *about* him.

Worship: Listen to "Through It All" performed by Hillsong.

Day 7

I DIDN'T SEE
THAT COMING

Word: Read John 16:33 and Matthew 6:31-34.

Summer driving in rural America usually means construction detours, road-blocks, and long lines waiting for a pilot car. When you have to travel ninety miles to an airport large enough to catch a flight on a real airline, it's a good idea to add time to your schedule… just in case. I had an important appointment in Los Angeles. Being a performing musician since I was sixteen, there was a hole in my life when I moved to a town with a population of 200 out in the middle of nowhere. I really felt like God wanted me to pursue my music for him, so I snagged an audition with a Christian record label in LA. It was a big deal. I packed the night before and left plenty of time for any detours. Then Murphy's Law kicked in.

About twenty-five miles down the road I missed the short cut to go "the back way." I can't even remember how I missed that turn. It was key to my plan. So plan B meant navigating the long way around on the highway. It was a half hour longer. My margin for error was shrinking. Then, I got stuck in a pilot car line. By the time I crept through the long stretch, I was way behind schedule. When I finally arrived at the airport parking lot my plane was boarding. In my rush I forgot my toiletries bag. With only an hour at my hotel before my audition, I was doomed to hotel hair products and no make-up. It seemed like the day couldn't get any worse.

So how do you rebound from that? The quality of our spiritual journey is going to be determined by how we handle what we didn't see coming. We like predictable; God likes detours. He's not trying to make our lives harder, just deeper and richer. If I want to be used by God, I must be willing to be disrupted. I must be willing to relinquish control. When we try and hang on to control, we are displacing God's work in our lives. We all need to take a lesson from Mary. Life is full of surprises. What are you going to do with them?

We may not always see it coming, but because we know disruption will come, we will not be surprised. Don't bother with the why—it will only derail you. Our job is to just embrace our life, to ask God to lead us through, and to always have our heart prepared for whatever comes our way. Let Jesus take the wheel; he knows the road you need to take.

Wait in prayer: Do you dread disruption? Write out a prayer asking God to help you see disruption as an invitation to go deeper with him and not as a negative. Ask him to help you to let go when trouble comes. Use Matthew 6:33-34 as an inspiration.

Worship: Listen to "Wanna Be Happy" performed by Kirk Franklin. For a treat, search for this song performed by Voices of Mobile on YouTube.

Day 8

LIVE LIKE YOU'RE A MEMBER OF THE ROYAL FAMILY

Word: Read 1 Peter 2:4-12.

In the first movie of the *Lord of the Rings* trilogy we meet Strider, who is really King Aragorn in hiding. Later in the movie we find that he was hidden as a child from the forces of evil that wanted to destroy his royal line. Even though he is of royal descent, he stayed in the shadows and joined the team of unlikely heroes protecting the ring of power from getting into the wrong hands. His royal heritage is still there, even though he doesn't claim his throne until the last movie in the series.

Sometimes I think we Christians are a little like Aragorn. Even though we have a royal inheritance, we live our lives totally unaware of the royal standing we have in Christ. When the enemy tries to take us out with a bout of disruption, we are tempted to forget who we are and whose we are. Remembering our royal blood is the anchor that keeps our hearts still when the waves start beating against the side of the boat. Remembering who we are in Christ helps us focus on the one from whom all things come (Romans 11:36).

Is this a point you struggle with? Do you consider your identity in Christ when you see trouble on the horizon? One of the best weapons we have to steer our reaction in the right direction is to remind ourselves that we are "a chosen people, royal priests, a holy nation, God's very own possession" (1 Peter 2:9). And what does a highly favored person do when times get tough?

Keep away from worldly desires that wage war against your very souls. Be careful to live properly among your unbelieving neighbors. Then even if they accuse you of doing wrong, they will see your honorable behavior, and they will give honor to God when he judges the world. (1 Peter 2:11-12 NLT)

Wait in prayer: Today, repeat the prayer from Ephesians 1:3-14 you learned in day four. Go back to it every day. Never, ever lose sight of who you are and whose you are.

"I am blessed in the heavenly realms with every spiritual blessing in Christ. I am chosen to be holy and blameless in Your sight. I am your adopted child. You've redeemed me from death. You've lavished your grace on me. You've made known to me the mystery of your will to me. I am marked with a seal guaranteeing my inheritance. You have forgiven my sins."

Worship: Listen to "I Am Who You Say I Am" performed by Hillsong Worship.

Day 9

TRYING WORRY ON FOR SIZE

Word: Read Philippians 4:6-7 and Ephesians 6:12-13.

I am a list maker. One of my top Strengths Finder© gifts is Strategic. Strategic people like to make plans, lists, and spreadsheets. I love contingency plans. My life motto should be "What if."

One of the lists we keep handy as believers is our list of objections. It has a heading on top that reads, "Please, God, Anything but This." It's a long list of things we don't want God to bring into our life. We're okay with a little disruption, but there are some lines we don't want God to cross. These are a list of our breaking points. But what this list actually does is invite a spirit of fear into our lives. Joyce Meyer used to call this a spirit of dread. But the truth is, God will not allow anything into our lives that is "more than we can stand" (1 Corinthians 10:13). God knows something about us that we do not. He knows right where our real breaking point is.

Sometimes he allows us to get dangerously close to that point, and sometimes we break because we get distracted by our list. Paul writes, "Finally, *be strong in the Lord and in His mighty power.* Put on the full armor of God, so that you can take your stand against the devil's schemes" (Ephesians 6:10-11, emphasis mine). All the items on your list are just schemes of the enemy. And God has given us some armor to stand against those schemes. The Bible doesn't promise that trouble won't hurt (is that on your list?) or that it won't bring grief (how about that?) but that we will be able to stand our ground (v. 13).

Wait in prayer: Take your list of objections and give it to Jesus. Ask him to sanctify it under his authority, giving over every item to him, and then pray to stand firm. It's a good idea to revisit the list occasionally if you feel those objections creeping back in. When they come to mind, remind yourself that God's got your list. I know it's hard to remember in the heat of the moment, but when we try on worry for size, God asks us to put on prayer instead (Philippians 4:6). Prayer is a one-size-fits-all garment for trouble. Write out Philippians 4:6-7 and personalize it. When we trust God with our worries, his peace guards our heart and mind in Jesus.

Worship: Listen to "It Is Well" performed by Kristene DiMarco.

Day 10

WHAT HAVE
I DONE NOW?

Word: Read Romans 8:1-2.

From the time David was anointed as the next king of Israel to the time he actually became king was twenty long years. Imagine you were promised a prestigious job promotion in a large company. After ten years and no promotion, would you start to lose heart? What about twenty? On top of that, the trouble David had to navigate was mind-blowing. King Saul wanted David dead.

Some days I feel like this is my life. How about you? You've got a dream. It might be a big one—something that seems impossible. But something you feel called to do. And the journey gets hard. So hard you start to think maybe you took a wrong turn on the path somewhere. But the truth is, the journey to our dreams is hard. There's proving to be done… and preparation for the next step.

One of the key truths we need to embrace about disruption is that it is not meant to punish or condemn us. Some part of our disruption may be a conviction—a call to let go of something or repent from something. But it is never a condemnation. Never. Romans 8:1 promises us that there is no condemnation for those who belong to Christ Jesus. Condemnation is shame's finger-wagging partner. Conviction is God's drawing love and grace. Condemnation is the work of our sinful nature pairing up with some lie. It's designed to draw us away, to discourage us. Don't let it. Call it out. Take that thought captive and hand it over to Jesus (2 Corinthians 10:3-5). And because we belong to him, the power of his Spirit in us sets us free from the power of that condemnation that leads to death. Disruption and detours are not our punishment. They are our road to better life.

Wait in prayer: Do you struggle believing that roadblocks in your life are God's punishment for something you did wrong? Write a personalized declaration from Romans 8:31-39 as a prayer of praise and thanksgiving and speak it out loud every day. Here is my personalized version from The Message I read the first thing in the morning or the last thing before I go to sleep. Keep yours on an index card next to your bed.

> *With God on my side, how can I lose? If God didn't hesitate to put everything on the line for me, a sinner, is there anything else he wouldn't gladly and freely do for me? And who would dare tangle with God by messing with me, one of God's chosen? The One who died for me—who was raised to life for me—he is in the presence of God at this very moment sticking up for me. Do you think anyone is going to be able to drive a wedge between me and Christ's love for me? There is no way! I'm absolutely convinced that nothing—nothing living or dead, angelic or demonic, today or tomorrow, high or low, thinkable or unthinkable—absolutely nothing can get between me and God's love because of what Jesus has done to set me free.*

Worship: Listen to "I Am Redeemed" performed by Big Daddy Weave.

Day 11

TWO ARE BETTER THAN ONE—FIND YOUR ELIZABETHS

Word: Read Hebrews 10:23-25 and Ecclesiastes 4:9-12.

In the 1990s, psychologist Robin Dunbar developed a method of defining the number of relationships we can sustain based on three factors: our brain's capacity, the time we have available to sustain those relationships, and our attention span. It's a formula known as Dunbar's number. His well-accepted research revealed several levels, or circles, of relationships that were defined by the number of people in each group. The first circle, labeled intimate friends, is made up of four to eight people. In *Women Finishing Well* we labeled this group our circle of influence.

After Mary got her news from Gabriel and a tip that her older relative Elizabeth was also expecting a miracle baby, she "hurried off to the hill country" to see her (Luke 1:36-45). She wasted no time building her circle of influence. She knew what was ahead and that she would need support and encouragement for the journey from a like-minded sister friend.

There are fifty-nine "one another" or "each other" Scriptures in the New Testament. God created us to thrive in community. We weren't meant to go it alone. We were meant to be at peace with one another, serve each other, pray for one another, love one another, be devoted to one another, honor one another above ourselves, and carry one another's burdens. And that is just the beginning. Mary needed Elizabeth to one another her through the coming nine or so months. Find the people that will stick with you no matter what. Disruption is easier to face when you do it with a close friend by your side. They will help you hold unswervingly to the hope you profess.

Wait in prayer: Can you write down the names of two to four women who know you inside out? Women who share life together, pray for each other, and keep each other accountable to God? Women who know how to one-another each other? If you don't have these women in your life, pray that God will help you start a list. Write down your first couple names and start praying. Everyday.

Worship: Listen to "I Will Be Your Friend" performed by Michael W. Smith.

Day 12

A LEAP OF FAITH REQUIRED

Word: Read Hebrews 11:1-3.

I have some fuzzy memories of the dark basement in our home as a young child. It was a damp underground cement fortress accessed by a set of rickety wooden stairs. The only time we ever used the basement was when there was a tornado warning. We would all hurry down the creaking stairs and sit on a blanket with a portable transistor radio, some flashlights, and a couple board games. Like a lot of little kids, the dark creeped me out. It's disconcerting not to be able to see if anything is lurking between you and a quick exit up the stairs.

In Hebrews 11 we see a list of heroes and heroines who stepped into the dark. The took a leap of faith like Indiana Jones off that ledge over the abyss. They had confidence in what they hoped for and assurance about what they could not see. They had faith in a God who created the universe. That was enough for them. They didn't need to see the exit. Disruption requires faith in what we cannot see. Detours require trusting when what's ahead is unknown.

Are you having a hard time seeing God in the dark times? God is not calling us to walk through the dark alone. We need to remember that God is standing *in* our dark. He abides in that unknown. He is reaching out his hand to walk us through. And he goes through beside us (Hebrews 13:5). Read that list again in Hebrews 11. Even in the dark, those people knew God was with them. So they took a leap of faith.

Wait in prayer: Are you afraid of the spiritual dark? Ask God to give you courage to take a step of faith into whatever he is calling you to do. Thank Jesus for walking beside you. He will never leave you or forsake you.

Worship: Listen to "Even If" performed by Mercy Me.

Day 13

FINDING NEW STRENGTH TO WAIT

Word: Read Isaiah 40:27-31.

I am one of those people who scouts for the shortest check-out line in the grocery store.

I am not good at waiting. Once I've made my mind up to do something, I want to move. But one thing I am learning over the years is that my anxiety doesn't make things move any faster. In Isaiah 40 we see the truth of the matter. We see that God "gives power to the weak and strength to the powerless. Even youths will become weak and tired, and young men will fall in exhaustion. But those who trust in the Lord will find new strength. They will soar high on wings like eagles. They will run and not grow weary. They will walk and not faint." (vv. 29-31 NLT). There are songs written about how those who hope in the Lord will renew their strength and fly like eagles. But what about verses 27-28? Isaiah asks Israel a question: Why do you say that God is not hearing you? Why do you say God is disregarding your cause? When we want God to act, if he doesn't do so right away, we think he's ignoring us. But Isaiah answers that lie right away in the next verses with sort of a sarcastic question: "Have you never heard? Have you never understood?" (v. 28, NLT).

I can feel the frustration in Isaiah's writing. I've been there. *Why isn't something happening, God?* Boy, that question gets me into trouble. But Isaiah continues: "The LORD is the everlasting God, the Creator of all the earth. He never grows weak or weary. No one can measure the depths of his understanding" (v. 28). And because God understands that we can lose heart, he adds, "He gives power to the weak and strength to the powerless. Even youths will become weak and tired. But those who trust in the Lord will find new strength" (vs. 29-31).

Not being able to wait is a weakness that God wants to turn into a *new strength*. God is always on duty, as my husband would say. He never takes a break. He doesn't run for coffee while you're in trouble. I can't always understand why he is asking me to wait, so I need to remember two things: God is not ignoring me, and his timing is perfect. And those who wait on him will soar on wings like eagles, run without getting weary, and not lose heart. Now that is worth waiting for.

Wait in prayer: Write out a prayer of confidence in God to turn your waiting into a new strength. Try personalizing the verses in Isaiah for inspiration. Ask God to help you to soar and not lose heart.

Worship: Listen to "Wait Upon the Lord" performed by Leeland.

Day 14

SOWING ON
THORNY GROUND

Word: Read Matthew 13:1-23 and 1 Peter 5:7.

One of the things I've learned in my forty-plus years as a farm wife is that all farmland is not created equal. Some soil is rich, some is poor, and some is too rocky to farm without running the rock picker over it every spring. But every year my husband and I seed every acre. Good soil, poor soil, rocky soil, and weedy soil each produce a different yield.

Like those different types of soil, our heart can have varying degrees of receptiveness to God's Word depending on how we've prepared it. This is masterfully illustrated by Jesus in the parable of the sower in Matthew 13. In that story the seed is the Word of God, and the various types of ground are the different levels of our heart's receptivity to that seed. There is the footpath, the rocky ground, the thorny ground, and the good soil. I encourage you to read the parable and journal your thoughts on what each type of ground represents. We're going to take a closer look at the thorny (or weedy) ground:

> The seed that fell among the thorns represents those who hear God's word, but all too quickly the message is crowded out by the worries of this life and lure of wealth, so no fruit is produced. (Matthew 13:22 NLT)

Did you catch that? No fruit. Not some fruit or stunted fruit but no fruit.

When we are chasing the cares of this world, we are sowing seeds on weedy ground. We are hoping that we can somehow mix God's truth with the lifestyle of our culture and the desire to have what everybody else has. No fruit will result. On the farm, some pieces of ground are better at growing weeds than wheat. If the ground is already infested with weed seeds and hasn't been properly prepared, weeds take over and the wheat dies (Matthew 13:7).

Worry and anxiety are weed seeds ready to choke anything that tries to sprout. But God has the solution for us in 1 Peter 5:7: "cast all your cares on him because he cares for you." We can take that sack full of worry seeds and hand it over to Jesus.

It's one thing to say but another thing to do. So how do we cast our worry on Jesus? Paul gives us some advice in Philippians 4:6-7. First, pray. About everything. Always present your requests to God first. And pray with thanksgiving because a grateful heart has a hard time being anxious. When we trust God with our worries, his peace will guard our hearts and minds in Christ Jesus. And a heart at peace with God is good soil.

Wait in prayer: Is there a disruption or a detour in your life right now that is tempting you to turn to the world for answers? Write out a prayer right now giving that request to God and thanking him for what he has done and what he has given you. Ask Jesus to help you leave that request with him. Ask the Holy Spirit to remind you when you try and reach out to take it back.

Worship: Listen to "Eye of the Storm" performed by Ryan Stevenson.

Day 15

THE SEASONS
OF LIFE

Word: Read Psalm 92:12-15 and Romans 12:1 (from The Message version).

I grew up in the Midwest where each calendar season has its own glorious beauty. I love the fall in Wisconsin. Watching trees turn shades of bright pink, deep crimson red, soft yellow, and dark purple blesses my soul. As a kid, I would collect some of the most beautiful leaf specimens, and my grandma would help me encase them in waxed paper with a warm iron. I put the dried leaves on the walls of my bedroom and loved glancing at their beauty throughout the barren months of winter.

Our lives have seasons that reflect creation, starting with the spring of youth and progressing to the quiet of a new snowfall in the winter. As I move through my autumn—I am now in my sixties—I am tempted to think that this season of my life is for slowing down. And maybe even that I'm disqualified from serving God in any impactful way. The world exalts the seasons of spring and summer and sometimes the church reflects that as well. But God has a plan for every season of our lives, and he wants us to embrace each season eagerly.

> Since my youth, God, you have taught me, and to this day I declare your marvelous deeds. Even when I am old and gray, do not forsake me, my God, till I declare your power to the next generation, your mighty acts to all who are to come. (Psalm 71:17-18)

God has been preparing us for autumn and winter since we were in spring. And the mission for each season has been the same since day one: declare God's power to the next generation. Declaring God's power to the next generation is a critical link in his plan. How we do that depends on the gifts, resources, and time God gives us. Where has he placed you in this season of life? Here's what he wants you to do:

> Take your everyday, ordinary life—your sleeping, eating, going-to-work, and walking-around life—and place it before God as an offering. Embracing what God has done for you is the best thing you can do for him. (Romans 12:1 MSG)

Embracing the everyday, ordinary life is the best thing we can do for him, no matter what season of life we are in.

Wait in prayer: What does your everyday, ordinary life look like? Read Romans 12:1 from The Message and make a list of your "walking around life." Where has God placed you? What gifts has he given you? Who are the people he has placed around you? Write a prayer asking God to help you embrace your everyday ordinary life. Ask him to open your eyes to the opportunities he puts in your everyday to speak love and life to those around you. If you just start there, you are on your way to living your best life for God.

Worship: Listen to "Come to the Table" performed by Sidewalk Prophets. The video for this song is a big blessing.

Day 16

CLIMBING
THE LADDER

Word: Read Philippians 3:4-8, Romans 12:2 (from The Message version).

One of the values our American corporate culture holds dear is "climbing the ladder." It's a figure of speech for working hard at the expense of friendships and family in exchange for power and higher income. This idiom has been the battle cry of the very wealthy since the 1950s. When we buy into this model, we are in for a life of dissatisfaction and emptiness. But what if the problem isn't the ladder, but the building we have the ladder up against?

When we prop our ladder against the world's building of success, every rung we climb is another step towards confidence in the flesh. Is God against success? Absolutely not. The Bible is filled with analogies about winning battles and reaching goals. God just wants us to have our ladder up against the right building. Move that ladder to God's kingdom and every step is another move toward embracing the abundant life God has given us. Climbing the ladder in God's kingdom will not leave you empty, but each step will fill you with a greater sense of God's purpose and joy in what he provides (1 Timothy 6:17-18).

Which building is your ladder leaning on?

Wait in prayer: Are there areas in your life where you are depending on yourself for success? Are there situations where the world is dragging you down to its level of maturity? Have you ever thought about how God can use your everyday, ordinary life to serve him successfully? Your eating, sleeping, going-to-work, and walking-around life to help build his kingdom? Write a prayer today based on Romans 12:1-2 from The Message version. Ask God to show you how the culture around you is dragging you down to its level.

Worship: Listen to "Riches" performed by Abagail Smith and Kingdom Culture Worship.

Day 17

BE A SERENDIPITY HUNTER

Word: Read John 4:4 and Hebrews 12:1-3.

When Jesus met the woman at the well in John 4, he wasn't just taking a short-cut back home. It was a divine detour that would change the lives of many in the town of Sychar. John tells us Jesus had to go through Samaria. He was on a recruiting mission. When we plan to do something and a detour pops up, our first reaction might be to heave a sigh and roll our eyes. Sometimes a detour is scary, sometimes it is an inconvenience. But hidden inside every detour is a serendipity—something that is a happy accident, a benefit we didn't expect. The woman at the well wasn't expecting anything out of the ordinary when she went to the well in the middle of the day. And I'm sure she never expected to be the first Christ-following missionary in the New Testament.

Hebrews 12:1 encourages us to throw off everything that hinders us and run with perseverance the race marked out for us. Hunting for serendipities on a detour takes perseverance. But if we expect them and look for them, we will find them. I could probably say with confidence that the woman's conversation with Jesus was probably the longest conversation she'd ever had with anyone. When Jesus spoke to her, she was drawn in. The longer their conversation went on, the more she was throwing off everything that hindered her: shame, fear, doubt. By the time he was done and the disciples showed up, she couldn't wait to run back to the village and proclaim that she had met the Messiah. She had discovered the unexpected benefit of speaking with Jesus: saving grace.

There is a gem from God in every detour you will face. It's there; don't give up. And the hunt for that serendipity makes the path we're running on smoother for us and for those coming behind us who need to discover that saving grace. What if the trials of your detours are your blessings in disguise?

Wait in prayer: Think back on a happy accident or unexpected benefit you discovered on a detour in your life. Write a prayer of thanks for the detour and ask God to give you the heart of a serendipity hunter every time you encounter a detour.

Worship: Listen to "Blessings" performed by Laura Story.

Day 18

BE A HEART
WHISPERER

Word: Read Colossians 4:5-6 and Galatians 5:13-15.

We live in an age where calling people out is an art form. Christians and non-Christians excel at criticizing others anonymously. One look at Twitter or Facebook is enough to make Pollyanna a cynic. Paul referred to this practice as biting and devouring one another (Galatians 5:15). He admonished his readers to remember that their freedom was not to be used to indulge in the flesh, but to serve one another in humble love "for the entire law is fulfilled in keeping this one command: Love your neighbor as yourself" (Galatians 5:14).

Scott Sauls, the senior pastor of Christ Presbyterian Church in Nashville, wrote in his book *The Gentle Answer* that Jesus knew how to talk to people's hearts and rarely pointed at their actions. In a world where hearts are heavy with shame and hopelessness that would be a good skill to have. We need to learn how to be heart whisperers like Jesus. A heart whisperer knows exactly how to answer everyone's needs. Our conversations should always be full of grace. We need to nourish one another (Colossians 4:6).

It's easy to speak our mind and give our opinion about anything and everything. Our conversation should be so flavorful and uniquely full of love and grace that people will know there is something different about us. Jesus is calling us to learn to draw people to God's love by listening to their hearts' need. Instead of needing to have the last word, we need to have the best word.

Wait in prayer: Write out a prayer asking God to help you learn how to make every conversation one that lifts up and encourages. Ask him to help you learn to answer hostility with gentleness and not to react to what you see. Ask him to help you forsake any us-against-them attitudes you might be hanging on to.

Worship: Listen to "Does Anybody Hear Her?" performed by Casting Crowns.

Day 19

THE LONGER
WAY AROUND

Word: Read Exodus 13:17-18, James 1:4.

Do you remember the days when we used to navigate road trips with actual paper maps? Every gas station had a display cabinet of maps for anywhere you were going from that point. I remember opening up huge folded maps in the back seat as a kid and looking at all the fascinating landmarks, lakes, and towns along the route. They were kind of clunky to look at while you were driving. Talk about distracted driving. These days, I am used to relying on Google Maps to show me the quickest way with one tap. And I can get frustrated when there's a detour. If Google says it should only take twenty-five minutes to get there, I'm cranky when it actually takes thirty-five.

In Exodus 13, after Pharaoh let Israel go, God did not lead them on the direct route to the promised land. The three-day direct route was through a country filled with warriors and armies. God knew Israel wasn't ready for battle yet, so he led them on a forty-year detour that began at the Red Sea. God was actually protecting Israel. They needed time to grow in courage and determination. The longer way around was going to be their proving ground.

Our journey to where God is leading us can sometimes feel like a wilderness. And that wilderness can be a refinery, the place where discomfort and pain take us closer to God. It could be that God is protecting you by taking you the long way around something in your life right now. Remember that the wilderness is not about the route; it's about the work God is doing in us. He is making us mature and complete, not lacking anything (James 1:4). The long way around is not a punishment—it's a preparation. When we persevere through those disruptions and detours, God will lead us to where we need to be to do what he has called us to do. Take heart, dear friend. If he is leading you through a dark valley, remember that it is filled with green pastures and still waters. Rest in it. Embrace his comfort (Psalm 23:1-4). He is the Good Shepherd. Goodness and mercy *will* follow you all the days of your life—even on the longer way around. Don't turn back; he will never let go of you.

Wait in prayer: Has God got you on a detour? Pray that you will feel his presence as you follow where he leads. Pray for perseverance as God works his will in you. Write out Psalm 23 as a personal prayer, replacing every "he" with "you" in verses one through three.

Worship: Listen to "You Never Let Go" performed by Matt Redman.

Day 20

STOP, LOOK, AND LISTEN

Word: Read 2 Thessalonians 3:16 and Psalm 34:14.

When my children were little, there was a popular curriculum in schools called Stop, Look, and Listen. Its main goal was to teach kids how to safely cross streets and railroad tracks. The first step was to *stop* whenever you wanted to cross a street or railroad tracks, whether you were chasing a ball or just standing at a crosswalk. Next, you were supposed to *look* both ways to see if you saw anything coming. Lastly, you were to *listen* for noise that indicated there might be something coming you couldn't see. If all the boxes were checked and nothing was coming, you were good to go. The object of the program was to get kids to stop, look, and listen first before crossing a street.

What is your first response to disruption? We can use the same stop, look, and listen mantra to help draw our attention back to the God of peace any time something unexpected comes across our path. First, *stop* and call on God. Ask him what's happening. Ask for wisdom—invite him into the disruption. Next, *look* at the situation. With God by our side, we won't be as distracted by troubles as instead we'll be looking at what is really going on. What are you actually feeling or seeing? What was the trigger? How does God want you to respond? And lastly, *listen* to how God is leading you. What do you need to do next?

The first thing we see in disruption is the need to take control. It stimulates an emotional response like fear or dread. Bring God in right away. Even if we're swirling around like a boat on a stormy sea, Jesus will speak peace to our hearts. What if our first response in trouble was to seek peace? When things are falling apart, look for the firm foundation. When things feel unstable, look for the solid Rock. When you feel hopeless, pursue the Hopeful One.

Wait in prayer: Write out a prayer to learn how to respond to trouble. You may want to borrow the stop, look, and listen formula. Ask God to help you learn to stop, look, and listen.

Worship: Listen to "Peace Be Still" performed by Hope Darst.

Day 21

WHEN IT IS
WHAT IT ISN'T

Word: Read John 10:10 and Genesis 3:1-7.

In our community in Arizona, the main boulevard is lined with beautiful orange trees. In the spring, they produce fragrant blossoms. I often stop on my morning walk, close my eyes, and breathe in the intoxicating scent. But these trees are not real orange trees. They produce a faux fruit that is so bitter you cannot use them for anything. They are called ornamental oranges.

It is so tempting to look at the world's definition of the abundant life and be taken in by the "fragrant" trappings. We're not talking about fairy tales here, just a nice little life: a modest home, a couple cars, kids who don't land in jail, a good-paying job, and a group of friends at church to hang out with. We are like Eve in the garden—taking it all in and seeing that it is pleasing to the eye (Genesis 3:6). But like Eve, if we start picking and eating that fruit, we are on the path to spiritual death. How can something that looks so good be so wrong?

Jesus warns us that the path to the abundant life is contrary to the path that the enemy wants us to take. Paul wrote to the Romans warning them not to "become so well-adjusted to your culture that you fit into it without even thinking. Instead, fix your attention on God. You'll be changed from the inside out. Readily recognize what he wants from you, and quickly respond to it. Unlike the culture around you, always dragging you down to its level of immaturity, God brings the best out of you, develops well-formed maturity in you" (Romans 12:2 MSG). God's idea of abundance is unlike the culture around us.

Sometimes it's hard to spot the fake. But the spiritual fake has bitter consequences. When we allow the culture around us to dictate the definition of abundant life, we are believing a lie. And when we believe a lie, we separate ourselves from God's best. Jesus' definition of abundant life in John 10:10 is found only in following him. And that may include disruption.

Today, make a decision to go on a hunt for that abundant life, not the ornamental version the world is offering. Live like you're loved.

Wait in prayer: Ask God to help you sort out what the abundant life looks like for you. Ask him if there are places in your life where you're settling for the fake. Thank him that richly provides everything for your enjoyment (1 Timothy 6:17-18).

Worship: Listen to "Live Like You're Loved" performed by Hawk Nelson.

Day 22

THE GOOD THING
I WANT TO DO—
KEEP IT SIMPLE

Word: Read Romans 7:15-20.

I used to think New Year's resolutions were a good idea. I mean, they are the perfect motivator for a person like me who likes goals and charts. For years I spent the last two weeks of every year pouring over the year before and prayerfully considering where I needed to be focusing my energies in the coming years. One year I even spent $300 on a course that was designed to help me do this more efficiently. Everything was going well until two years later when I had some major life changes. The course's system didn't allow for interruptions of that magnitude. I sort of lost my motivation the following December to tackle the whole process again.

Then I read a book by Robert D. Smith called *20,000 Days and Counting*, and I realized that the most important thing in life to master was today. In that short, power-packed book I learned more about following God than any Bible study I had read up to that point. I learned that I could not plot out the perfect Christian life (surprise surprise), and no amount of goal setting or spread-sheeting was going to get me there. Thanks to Robert D. Smith, I can tell you exactly how many days old I am—I put it in my journal every day.

Paul had a zest for living for today that was unparalleled in the Bible. On any given day he didn't know if he was going to be thrown in jail, stoned, or called before the highest authority in the land to preach the gospel. And he didn't care. He just took what came and did what he was called to do with every ounce of energy he had. Paul wasn't perfect, and he knew it. He understood the pull sin has on us after we are saved when he wrote:

> I do not understand what I do. For what I want to do I do not do, but what I hate I do. And if I do what I do not want to do, I agree that the law is good. As it is, it is no longer I myself who do it, but it is sin living in me. For I know that good itself does not dwell in me, that is, in my sinful nature. For I have the desire to do what is good, but I cannot carry it out. For I do not do the good I want to do, but the evil I do not want to do—this I keep on doing. Now if I do what I do not want to do, it is no longer I who do it, but it is sin living in me that does it. (Romans 7:15-20)

In this passage he is telling us that we have to recognize that sin's pull still lives in us. We never get rid of that sinful nature. It is with us fighting every step of the way until we die. We are human. We don't want to follow its desire, but sometimes we do. And that is not failure because God knows we can't be perfect. That's why Jesus died for us. He didn't die to give us sinless perfection, just a way back when we need forgiveness.

Friend, if you are a Christ follower, if you've trusted Jesus to be your Savior from sin and desire to live a life fully dedicated to following where he leads, then you're good. Just keep on keeping on. Life has disruptions. We screw up. People we love leave. We can't make heaven on earth, but we can set our hearts on things above where Christ is seated at the right hand of God… and he is smiling down on us. You don't need to be perfect. God just wants your heart. Keep it simple.

Wait in prayer: Today, write out a prayer thanking God for sending Jesus, so you don't have to be perfect. Ask God to help you not get discouraged when you don't do the good thing you want to do. Ask him to help you embrace your everyday ordinary life one day at a time.

Worship: Listen to "Love God, Love People" performed by Danny Gokey.

Day 23

THERE IS
A WAY OUT

Word: Read 1 Corinthians 10:12-13.

I have not had a good experience with a corn maze. As a matter of fact, I've only had one experience, and it was enough that I never wanted to do it again. So if you're asking me if I would recommend that as a nice leisurely autumn activity, I would say no—especially not at night.

My one experience started out well enough. We had a guide, but she got lost. It was a big maze, and our guide didn't have a walky-talky. And did I mention that I was leading a church youth group activity? Have you ever been stuck in a small pitch black space with a bunch of frightened, screaming teenage girls? At least their screaming got us found. That was about the only good thing that happened that night.

Sometimes when we're caught in the darkness of sin, it can feel like we are lost in a maze in the pitch black of night. There are lots of choices. We know one them is the right way, but we can't tell the good from the bad from the ugly. Thankfully, there is a way out. But we have to stop, look, and listen.

Paul puts our choices in perspective in his letter to the Corinthians: "The temptations in your life are no different from what others experience. And God is faithful. He will not allow the temptation to be more than you can stand. When you are tempted, he will show you a way out so that you can endure" (1 Corinthians 10:13 NLT).

I can't always find my way in the darkness of life—especially if there is fear, indecision, or shame involved. But thankfully I have a Guide who does not need a walky-talky to find the right exit. You know what? God does not want to see you fail. He provides a way out. And if we look for the way out, we will find it. It may take some backtracking and winding around where you've been before, but you'll get there. God's got you surrounded.

Wait in prayer: Write out a prayer thanking God for providing a way out when you need one. You may want to write out 1 Corinthians 10:13 and personalize it. Memorize it so that when you're in the dark and hit a dead end or can't find the exit, you can reach out to the true Guide.

Worship: Listen to "Surrounded (This is How I Fight My Battles)" performed by Michael W. Smith.

Day 24

HOW THE
GARDEN GROWS

Word: Read John 15:1-8 and Hebrews 12:11.

Tending a garden is a big commitment. Whether it's just tomato plants in patio pots or a full-blown backyard vegetable garden that provides a pantry of canned goods, it's a chore. When I first started gardening as a young wife, I wanted to plant everything. We had lots of spare room in the yard, so I asked my husband to till a huge spot near our water supply. The next spring I had had my blueprint and seeds ready to go. It took me a few days to get everything planted, but when I was done, I beamed with excitement about the new grocery store growing in our yard. It took me two weeks to realize I had over-extended myself. Weeds, watering, fertilizing, and bugs became my full-time occupation. I was now a full-time gardener whether I liked it or not.

Jesus teaches us that spiritual growth is like a garden—a work in progress. It can happen in spurts, while we're waiting in the desert, and when we have to take three steps backward and re-think. In John 15, Jesus tells us we are the branches. As gardeners know, branches cannot survive apart from the plant. As branches, we have to remain attached to the vine in order to bear fruit because apart from the vine we can do nothing, And Jesus said he is the true vine and his Father is the gardener. No matter how many Bible studies we attend, how many Sundays in a row we go to church, or how much money we tithe, we won't survive without a vital, living relationship with Jesus. He said that if we do not remain in him, we will wither and die (John 15: 5-6). So how do we remain in him? Jesus said, "If you keep my commands, you will remain in my love, just as

I have kept my Father's commands and remain in his love" (John 15:10). And what command was he specifically referring to? "Love each other as I have loved you" (v. 12). No long list of works to do, just something simple but not easy.

As you wind up your time with this book, there is one thing I hope you will take to heart: there is no growth without disruption or pruning. It can be painful, but afterward it produces a harvest of righteousness (Hebrews 12:11). God is our gardener. Jesus is the vine. Stay connected to the source of life and the gardener will make sure you will grow exceedingly, abundantly, over and above all you dare ask or think (Ephesians 3:20).

Wait in prayer: Read John 15:1-8 and write out a prayer confessing to God's work in your life and committing to stay plugged into Jesus, the source of your life. Acknowledge his love you for you and thank him for his protection. Let him know that apart from him, you can do nothing.

Worship: Listen to "You Have Made Me Glad" performed by Hillsong

Day 25

EVERYDAY ORDINARY TROUBLE IS THE PROVING GROUND

Word: Read Matthew 6:34, 1 Corinthians 10:13, and Romans 12:1 (from The Message).

About two hundred miles west of Phoenix lies the nation's largest military proving ground—one of the biggest military installations in the world. The Yuma Proving Ground includes over thirteen hundred square miles of land. The climate and location make it the perfect location for testing every ground combat weapon in the US military arsenal. Its remote desert terrain is the perfect practice spot for everything from unmanned helicopters to tanks to land mine systems.

The proving ground is the military's safety net. A proving ground is a place that demonstrates whether a weapon really works or not. It's where they can test the equipment before it's needed. Can you imagine what devastation might occur if soldiers were sent into the battlefield with faulty weapons?

God has given us a proving ground for our faith. It's called our everyday, ordinary life. When we embrace the little disruptions that come into our lives— the spills at breakfast, the red lights on the way to work, or the slow clerk checking you out—then we are ready to face the bigger challenges. In our everyday challenges—like when the hubby says he's busy watching football so he can't take the garbage out—is where we learn how to take thoughts captive. Trivial challenges are where habits are made. When the car won't start and we have a doctor's appointment, how do we react? When we see a hateful remark about a friend on social media, what is our first response? When your daughter is the only classmate left out of the slumber party, what do you tell her? The little things are the proving ground.

Remember 1 Corinthians 10:13? Every temptation has a way out. Every trouble has an exit door. Jesus said in Matthew 6:34 that every day has plenty of trouble. Do you let disruptions send you into a tailspin? When your girlfriend is thirty minutes late picking you up for a movie, do you get edgy with each minute that passes? If you take one thing with you from this book, let it be that our everyday ordinary lives have sufficient amounts of trouble to produce spiritual growth. And embracing those everyday, ordinary disruptions is the best thing we can do for God. The. Best. Thing.

Wait in prayer: Do you really believe that everyday ordinary troubles are your faith's proving ground? Write out the following version of Romans 12:1 from The Message and memorize it. It's one of the most effective daily prayers you can pray, if you pray it from the heart. I guarantee it will make a huge difference in your spiritual growth when you start to walk it out.

"So here's what I'm going to do, God. I'm taking my everyday ordinary life, my sleeping, eating, going-to-work, and walking-around life—and placing it before you as an offering. Trouble or no trouble, I know embracing whatever you bring me is the best thing I can do for you."

Worship: Listen to "I Will Follow" performed by Chris Tomlin.

Day 26

DON'T LOOK DOWN

Word: Read Matthew 14:22-33.

In Matthew 14 Jesus had just fed thousands of people with five loaves and two fishes. After the disciples picked up the leftovers, Jesus told them to get in a boat and go to the other side without him. After their boat was a considerable distance out, the wind came up and the waves started to rock the boat. Now there were a few fishermen in this boat, so I don't imagine they were scared; just focused. To navigate choppy waters you need to concentrate on the movement of the boat against the wind. When Jesus came to their boat walking on the water, they were terrified (Mathew 14:26). Now they had two sets of troubles at once: the rocking boat and someone walking on the water they thought might be a ghost.

But when Peter recognized Jesus on the water, he had enough courage to ask to walk on the water as well. Jesus didn't give him any instructions; he didn't test the wind speed or look to see if Peter's clothing was too heavy. He just said, "Come."

Peter got out of the boat and started walking. Then he did the one thing we do sometimes when we're in troubled waters—he looked down, saw the wind and the waves, and began to sink. Instead of keeping his eyes focused on the miraculous presence of Jesus, he looked at his challenge. In that moment Jesus reached out his hand and caught him (v. 31).

Is there something you're going through right now that feels like a rocking boat in a wind storm? Don't doubt Jesus. He is standing there right with you, calling you. Don't take your eyes off him. If you get distracted by the waves, look up. He is there to catch you when you start sinking.

Wait in prayer: Write out this personalized prayer from Deuteronomy 31:6 and put it on your list of Scripture prayers to memorize: I will be strong and courageous. I will not be afraid or terrified, for you are with me, Jesus. I know you are with me wherever I go. I thank you that you will never leave me or forsake me.

Worship: Listen to "Waymaker" performed by Michael W. Smith.

Day 27

FIRST THINGS FIRST

Word: Read Hebrews 4:12 and Matthew 7:24-27.

I was engaged in a robust conversation the other day with a friend about how our kids don't seem to know much about the Bible. It seems her husband mentioned to their adult son that a certain TV show might not be appropriate for their young children. Like many of these generational conversations go, the elders tend to point to the Bible, and the youngers, even though they were brought up in a Bible-teaching home, sometimes think that the Scriptures are too strict. But what struck me was when my friend admitted that neither one had any actual Biblical evidence for their opinions.

Today, more than ever before, the Word of God needs to be embedded in our *lives* not just in our speech. In Matthew 7:24-27, Jesus talks about the wise builder and the foolish builder. But most people I talk to remember this as a parable of the foundations—the sand and the rock. We know that the rock is a life built on following God and the sand is, well, foolish. But let's dig a little deeper into this parable. It isn't just about knowing what the Bible says and being able to use that in an argument. What Jesus was really getting at here is found in verse 26: "Everyone who hears these words of mine and does not put them into practice is like a foolish man who built his house on sand." I truly believe there are a lot of professed Christians who fit this verse. According to a Lifeway Research report, 12 percent of church goers in the U.S. rarely or never read their Bible. The same report said less than one-third of the whole group surveyed reads the Bible regularly. It's probably hard to put into practice what you don't read regularly.

In the book *Women Finishing Well*, we encourage our readers and podcast listeners to adopt a routine we call First Things First. It's a daily practice of five disciplines you can do in about ten to fifteen minutes that connects you to God directly. It is imperative that Christ followers learn how to follow Jesus through a personal, interactive relationship with God's Word. Why? Because a closer relationship with the Word opens the lines of communication between us and God's Spirit in us. It allows God to speak directly into our lives; to lead us and guide us in the way we should go. (Ps. 32:8) It is about a relationship with the living God.

> For the word of God is alive and active. Sharper than any double-edged sword, it penetrates even to dividing soul and spirit, joints and marrow; it judges the thoughts and attitudes of the heart. (Hebrews 4:12)

Notice that the Word of God is capable of dividing our souls from our spirit. It is that precise and sharp. The Word judges our attitudes and helps us discern right from wrong. Without reading the Bible that discernment is all guess work.

To go deeper we God, consider a daily morning routine that will keep your heart and mind sharp and connected with God. I call these disciplines the 5 Ws:

- **Wake-up call:** First thing in the morning before you get out of bed pray a prayer that focuses on God's faithfulness and commits the day to him. It can be as long or short as you like.

- **Water:** Before you put any caffeine or sugar or other substances in your body, drink a glass of water—cold or warm, it doesn't matter. It has numerous health benefits that include a clearer mind.

- *Word:* Using the SOAP method have a short study of God's Word to interact with a passage of your choice. Or, use one of the many reading plans available in many places including the *YouVersion* Bible app.

- *Wait in prayer:* Prayer and reflection on what you've studied and intercession for requests on your heart.

- *Worship:* End with some sort of praise—reading a psalm or listening to a worship song on YouTube, Pandora, or Spotify.

If you're interested in running through a short mini study on the 5 Ws, you can access one for free on the Women Finishing Well website here: https://womenfinishingwell.com/first-things-first-free-tool/. Once you start this daily habit, you'll never look back. Remember, if this is new to you, start slow—maybe ten minutes a day. There are an abundance of tools and resources both online and offline in this short look at starting a daily time with God.

Wait in prayer: Ask God to help you start a new personal habit of regular Bible study. If you already read and study regularly, ask God to take you deeper. Ask God to help you be faithful—and if you miss a day, remember God is always there waiting for you to come back. More than anything, he wants to reveal his heart to you in his Word.

Worship: Listen to "Your Word" performed by Hillsong

Day 28

PLAYING THE
LONG GAME

Word: Read James 1:3-4 and Romans 8:28.

When I was a new Christian, I was so enthusiastic about God. I couldn't get enough of Jesus. I was blessed with close like-minded Christian women friends who were my age. We would get together and talk about our hopes and dreams of serving God. Then life happened.

One day I was driving down the road with my closest friend, and we began ruminating about how the Christian life sometimes felt like a slog. "Yeah," she said. "We're just looking for that life of ease, aren't we? Where is that abundant life anyway?" We had made the classic mistake of misunderstanding the abundant life. We were trying to put together events, relationships, and even moments that were evidence that God really loved us. But they were so mixed in with the cares of life that we couldn't see what was right in front of us: God present in our everyday, ordinary lives.

The abundant life is not our creation; it is embracing who God created us to be. The abundant life is not a formula; it is a process of following where God leads, clearing out the underbrush one section at a time. It's a long game that is filled with blessings *and* troubles. Those two are not separated—remember Romans 8:28? All things work together to form the abundant life God has for us.

Are you willing to grow with the good and the bad? For the rest of your life? Do you believe that God's best for you is sometimes forged in trouble? Life with God is a mixture of high points, normality, and disruptions. When we finally get to the place where we embrace the life God has given us, God is blessed. Rise up. God's love for you is right here, right now. In all of it.

Wait in prayer: Do you believe the abundant life is a long game dotted with detours and disruptions? If you haven't done this already, write out a personalized version of James 1:2-4. I like the New Living Translation for these verses. Get yourself some colored index cards and write this out on several cards of different colors. Put one in your purse, one on your refrigerator, one on your bathroom mirror, one in your car, one on the inside of your door to the outside. Put one anywhere you'll see it. Say it out loud every time you see it. I recommend doing this for at least thirty days. But always keep one in your purse and on your bathroom mirror. Remember, you're playing the long game.

Worship: Listen to "Rise Up" performed by Matt Maher.

Day 29

DON'T FORGET
THE BECAUSE

Word: Read Habakkuk 3:17-19.

Dental work is my nemesis. I dread the appointment for days. I've never been a big fan of mouth pain. Even a routine cleaning throws me for a loop. I've always had a hard time remembering to floss. When I shared that with my dentist, he told me, "Oh, you don't have to floss your teeth every day." Shocked at this new revelation, I answered, "Really?" And he glibly answered, "Only the ones you want to keep."

Knowing the why behind the task makes it more real for me. Just telling me to floss every day for good mouth health, whatever that is, wasn't very motivating. "You're going to lose your teeth" was the clincher.

In our journey to embrace the disruptions and detours God brings our way, we need to know the *why* behind the pain. Some scholars believe the short book of Habakkuk was written to prepare the people for captivity by the Babylonians. At the end of this book of oracles, Habakkuk writes a prayer that contains the three necessary declarations of making it through disruption with our faith strengthened: though, yet, and because.

"*Though* the fig tree does not bud and there are no grapes on the vines though the olive crop fails and the fields produce no food, though there are no sheep in the pen and no cattle in the stalls…" (3:17, emphasis mine). There is nothing good on this list, so we know the prophet is setting us up for how to deal with trouble.

"*Yet* I will rejoice in the LORD, I will be joyful in God my Savior" (3:18, emphasis mine). Now these two verses together represent a statement of faith about trouble. They are comforting. But they are also perplexing. How is this possible?

"The Sovereign LORD is my strength; *he* makes my feet like the feet of a deer, *he* enables me to tread on the heights" (3:19, emphasis mine). When we add the *because*, we understand that it is possible to rejoice in trouble. Not because of what we believe, but because of who he is.

Friend, it's one thing to know what the Bible promises, and another great thing to *believe* it's true. But until we accept that this life of faith is only possible because of who God is, we just have some promises on paper. They are true because the one who promised is True. Never, ever forget the because.

Wait in prayer: Is it possible that our faith can be in our faith and not in our God? If I just believe, will it be true? Confess to God that your faith is in him, not in what you believe. Thank him for his power at work within you, for his intervention of blessings and trouble in your life. Ask him to help you see disruption for what it really is—an opportunity to get closer to him. And ask him to help you really believe.

Worship: Listen to "I Believe (The Creed)" performed by Hillsong Worship.

Day 30

NO-HOLDS-BARRED

Word: Read Romans 12:2 (from The Message version).

The act of wrestling is over 15,000 years old. It was first referenced in cave drawings as a method of hand-to-hand combat. The modern sport of wrestling evolved through many iterations but was one of the sports mentioned in the ancient Olympic games. The rules of the sport governing the types of holds that were illegal and could disqualify a competitor also evolved over the years. In the 1800s, wrestling became a mainstream form of entertainment, and you could take in a respectable match at the opera house, or one not so respectful match in a local dive bar where the free form of no-holds-barred wrestling could include a fight to the death. The tagline of the 1989 movie of the same name read: "No Ring. No Ref. No Rules."

Modern Christianity has a lot of rules. Rules about what a good Christian looks like. Rules about what a good Christian church looks like. Rules about what a good Christian woman looks like. And so on. There is always going to be a brand of Pharisee-influenced faith that makes so much noise it gets tough to hear God. Add to that the hectic pace we all live and it's no wonder we can't discern the Spirit moving in our lives. It's like God is in the background not the foreground where he belongs. Maybe Carlos Whittaker was right when he wrote in *Enter Wild* that we need to lower the volume of our lives so the volume of God can go up.

Keeping all the rules takes a lot of time and energy. What if we took that time and energy to just slow down and listen? To read and pray more? To shut off the TV and power down the phones for just a couple hours at the end of the day? What if we decided to follow Jesus with a no-holds-barred attitude?

Good Christians don't have trouble. That's the first rule we need to get rid of. There, I said it. Jesus said, "I have told you these things so that in me, you may have peace. In this world *you will have trouble*. But take heart! I have overcome the world" (John 16:33). Jesus is busting all the holds on the abundant life. In the first half of John 10:10 he identifies the truth: the thief comes to kill, steal, and destroy. And in the second half of that verse he gives us the keys: "I came that they may have life and have it abundantly."

Wait in prayer: Are there any "holds" in your life that are keeping you from going all-in and answering the call of God to a more abundant life? Do you have a bag of excuses like Moses? A bullying friend or family member like Hannah? A career path like Paul that is drawing you away from God? We're going to end our thirty days together with a personalized prayer from Romans 12:2 (from The Message version). Memorize it. It will help you recognize when the world has a stranglehold on your life. That's an illegal hold, by the way.

> O God, don't let me become so well-adjusted to my culture that I fit into it without even thinking. Instead, help me fix my attention on you, God. I invite you to change me from the inside out. Holy Spirit, help me readily recognize what You want from me, and quickly respond to it. Unlike the culture around me that always drags me down to its level of immaturity, you, God, bring the best out of me. You develop well-formed maturity in me. Teach me to listen.

Worship: Listen to "Chain Breaker" performed by Zach Williams.

Appendix One

LEADER'S GUIDE

Leading a Bible study can be a huge blessing *and* a monumental challenge. In this first section I am going to share some tips that have helped me over the years.

BEFORE THE FIRST SESSION

Never get discouraged. If you feel leading a study is something God wants you to do, then go for it. Just remember that the leader's enthusiasm sets a tone for the group. Having said that, I will caution you that your group members may have varying levels of enthusiasm and commitment throughout the course of the study. We often start out with great expectations and then life happens. You've made a big step to help them get closer to God and get to know each other better. Embrace the process!

- *Don't let the fact that some don't do their "homework" be a cause for discouragement.* Encourage every woman to come every week and never stay home if she doesn't complete the assignments. The important thing isn't the work, it's the connection with other women. Some of us are doers and some are observers. We can grow either way.

- *Don't worry about overcommunicating meeting times and what lesson you're doing this week.* I have all my Bible study women on an email program, and I email them all twice every week during our study. You can make a list with an email carrier like Yahoo or Gmail as well. The first goes out the day after we meet thanking everyone and reminding them where we are meeting next, what time, and what lesson we're doing along with anything they're asked to bring. I send out basically the same email the day before we meet.

- *It's best to distribute the study books ahead of the first meeting or have them buy their own, whichever you prefer.* Encourage them to peruse the book—maybe read the introduction, table of contents, and about the author.

- *Decide if you're going to meet in one location throughout or move around to different homes.* Decide what day of the week and time works best for everyone. Schedule a beginning and ending time.

YOUR FIRST MEETING

Try and personally welcome everyone as they arrive. Use name tags if the women don't know each other.

- You may choose to use your first meeting as a welcome week and not have any assigned homework. I recommend this option as it gives you a chance to create some community and explain the in's and out's of the material and how your weekly meetings will go. Here are some of the topics you may want to cover.

  - Consider providing refreshments. I recommend this not be elaborate, especially if you are moving around to different people's homes. Keep it simple: coffee, water, tea, sparkling waters. Set an example that will be easy for every host to duplicate.

  - Always start on time to honor those that are there on time. I like to start my sessions with some kind of short ice breaker that gets people visiting and talking and allows for late comers to not feel like they are interrupting.

  - At this first meeting consider playing some ice breakers that will help everyone feel comfortable.

  - Take a few minutes to let everyone introduce themselves and give them a question to answer like, "tell us about your favorite hobby."

— Take some time to go through the format of the study. Talk about the importance of using journals to interact with each chapter's lesson. Bring some information about where they can purchase journals (Target, Staples, online, etc). Draw attention to the Journal Points and Digging Deeper exercise at the end of each chapter. Draw their attention to Appendix 2 and make sure everyone understands how to use the SOAP method of study. Be ready to answer questions. Be prepared.

— Encourage them to do all the weekly homework but encourage them to come even when they don't have time to do it. Make sure they know that each meeting is a safe zone where they can come as they are.

— If you have women in your group that are using an ebook version of the study I encourage you to get a copy of the ebook (email me if you want a link to one for free) and put it on your laptop or phone. You will need to install the free Kindle reading app on your phone or computer if you haven't got it already. Just Google "kindle reading app" and you'll find a free download page. That way, when people reference page numbers of a print book, you can help the ebook people know where that reference point is. My email is below and you can email me with any questions.

DISCUSSION GUIDELINES:

Encourage everyone to participate but don't put anyone on the spot. Be prepared to offer answers to questions if no one else responds at first.

- A leader is more of a guide. Don't dominate the conversation. Make an effort to steer conversation that drives engagement.

- If someone is monopolizing the conversation, thank her for her answer and then ask for others to weigh in.

- Don't rush into silence. Sometimes a question needs some thought. Encourage good discussion but don't be afraid to move on to keep the group on track.

- Do your best to end on time. If you are running over, let members know they are free to go. Try to leave at least 10 or 15 minutes at the end to pray. Be prepared if some women want to stick around.

LEADER PERSONAL HELP

If you have any questions about any of the material in the study, please feel free to email me and ask a question. My email is chris@womenfinishingwell.com. Also, stay tuned to our Women Finishing Well Facebook page where we will be doing Facebook Live videos for leaders occasionally. Just search for Women Finishing Well on Facebook.

Appendix Two

USING THE SOAP METHOD TO STUDY THE BIBLE

One of the simplest, yet most effective ways to study your Bible is using the acronym SOAP. The method includes four parts that are best done in order. Each step is a letter from the SOAP acronym. The process can be as simple or elaborate as you have time for. I recommend using a journal to keep track of your studies.

> S = Scripture
>
> O = Observation
>
> A = Application
>
> P = Prayer

Let's take a quick look at what each of these pieces looks like.

- **Scripture:** In your journal, write the Scripture reference you'll be studying. It might be from a reading plan, a daily devotional, a Bible study, or a particular passage you're interested in. If you're just beginning, I recommend you start with a devotional reading plan like one of the apps in chapter four on page 29. I've included a short list of paperback devotionals in the First Things First section of this chapter for those of you that prefer a hard copy.

- **Observation:** What jumps out at you in this passage? Who is talking? Who is the audience? What comes right before and after the

passage you are reading? If you are using a devotional or reading plan, there may be a reading that comments on the passage. If
you've read this passage before, did you see anything new?

- **Application:** How does this apply to you? This is where the verses
  become personal. Listen. Is the Holy Spirit drawing your mind to
  a particular change or action you need to take? Is there a truth that
  you can take away to begin working into your life?

- **Prayer:** Is there a way you can personalize a prayer from this Scripture? Ask God to give you wisdom about this passage and bring it
  to your mind throughout the day. If there is sin to confess, do it
  now. If there is something to work into your life today, ask God to
  hold you accountable. Thank Him.

"Those who love your instructions have great peace and do not stum-
ble. I long for your rescue, LORD, so I have obeyed your commands.
I have obeyed your laws, for I love them very much. Yes, I obey your
commandments and laws because you know everything I do." (Ps.
119:165-168, NLT)

ENDNOTES

Chapter One: The Mistaken Identity

1. Carlos Whittaker, *Enter Wild* (Colorado Springs: WaterBrook Multnomah, 2020).

Chapter 3: No Ifs, Ands, Or Buts

1. Indiana Jones and the Last Crusade (Directed by Steven Spielberg, 1989). "Leap of Faith," https://www.youtube.com/watch?v=YpzBQamQpk0.

2. "William Wilberforce," Christian History, Christianity Today, https://www.christianitytoday.com/history/people/activists/william-wilberforce.html.

Chapter 4: Yes, But—Clauses, Conditions, And Caveats

1. "Hatred Between Jews and Samaritans," The Word in Life Study Bible, New Testament Edition, (Thomas Nelson Publishers, Nashville; 1993), pp. 340-341, https://bible.org/illustration/hatred-between-jews-and-samaritans.

2. Mount Sinai, by Joseph Jacobs, M. Seligsohn, Wilhelm Bacher, Jewish Encyclopedia, http://www.jewishencyclopedia.com/articles/13766-sinai-mount#anchor1.

3. Goff, Bob. *Live in Grace, Walk in Love*. Nelson Books, 2019.